The

Unwelcome Committee

Lee,
Thank you for
your love and support!
Healing Happens,
Khadija

THE
UNWELCOME COMMITTEE

Chasity Williams

Maureen Bobo

Khadija Ali

Copyright

Published by Create Space Publishing

Printed in the United States of America

DEDICATION

This book is dedicated to the memory of:

Darrell N. Williams

Martin Bobo

A. Karriem Ali

Rebecca Victoria Teague Paige

Jack Sage (PawPaw Jack)

Fred Banks (Papa Banks)

Jeannie Cox

Table of Contents

FOREWORD

Death is a part of the cycle of life. We are born with the expectation of living a long life. And after we live that life, then comes death. We all know that life doesn't always work that way. When your life is turned upside down by tragedy, you begin to wonder how you will go on.

As a child who lost her father at a very young age, I know how death can affect you. I was a little girl lost because I no longer had access to my father. I remember thinking, *did I do something wrong? Did God take him because of me?* My friends, they had their fathers, but I felt alone, abandoned. Growing up, it was always about how my father's death affected me. I never really thought much about my mother in all of this.

The authors of this book, Khadija, Maureen, and Chasity, will take you on a personal journey of how difficult life can be after death. There are so many areas of life that are crossed when death happens. This is not just a book for spouses who have lost someone but the children that are left behind. Reading their stories allowed me to see just what my own mother must have been feeling not having that father to look to for help.

This book will allow you to look at that person you know who is dealing with the loss of a spouse, in a different light. You will have a better understanding of their grief, isolation, financial struggle, life balance, and ability to take care of the kids. The Unwelcome

Committee is more than a book; it was an eye opener that I had the privilege to read.

Thank you, ladies!

Christina Saunders, Christian life coach

www.lostnfoundu.com

PREFACE

Maureen

There is an expectation that grief should conform to a general pattern or principle. Reading this book, you will see this is not the case. I'm hoping this book is as therapeutic to those who read it as it was to us who wrote it. It's a needed resource guiding a hurting soul through the murkiness that is grief. I have had the privilege to share this widow's walk with Khadija Ali and Chasity Williams. Through all the ups, downs, backwards, and forwards of this journey they have been consistent with this project. I love them very much as my sisters in sorrow. Ultimately, this book is a ministry of love to those coming behind us on this path. I truly believe that.

Khadija

We began this journey on September 16, 2012, with ten widows who were at various stages of their journey. The intention was to have many stories included in the book to give readers a variety of stories to relate to. As time progressed, some of the original members could not handle reliving their stories, others simply dropped off and resumed their lives without explanation, and then suddenly, there were only three left. I tell this story not to condemn anyone or judge but to simply say that we have stood the test of time with writing this book. We could write a book about writing this book (smile). We survived intense arguments and disagreements, not speaking to each other on occasion, illness, and just plain ole life happenings. This book is truly something special, and it is our hope that we inspire and give hope to those of you who are, unfortunately, coming behind us.

Chasity

This book is not only relatable for just losing a spouse, but a resource to understand the perspective of grief overall and to educate. You will understand where we were personally, the roller coaster of emotions that it brings, the "split personality" we tend to have, and how it took a lot of time to get where we are years later. The book includes an abundant of topics that anyone dealing with grief could relate. Starting from the insensitivity of friends and family, isolation, personal and social anxiety, reality vs. society's expectations, a new normal, digression, rage and resentment, sadness, unanswered questions we will never receive, parenting and dealing with their milestones without their parent, gaining to be understood and most importantly learning to be a new 'you' aside from being a spouse and parent. The book is raw, uncut and has a lot of personal reflections you may be surprised to read. We chose to share our stories so if just one person needs someone to relate to and understand them without judging and expectations then we will be blessed. Although, writing this book took an extensive four years, I can only hope it will touch many; if not I am okay with that too; writing it and collaborating with my coauthors was tremendously therapeutic. This book is not only for people who need it, but also for my family and friends to really grasp why I did a lot of things I did or did not do. Grief is a monster and sadly everyone will have to deal with it sooner or later in his or her life. You never get over your loved one being gone and the grief, but you learn a better way to get through it! The hole in your heart may mend, but there will always be a scar.

ACKNOWLEDGEMENTS

Chasity

I would like to express my gratitude to the following people:

My husband Darrell Williams who we will always hold a special place in my heart and mind. You were my first love and I will always love you. Your love, legacy and memories will always be cherished and never be forgotten. PS- Look at our boy and go Cowboys!!

Khadija and Maureen, for countless conference calls, conversations, tears, laughs, private sharing, the time, holding each other accountable, and most importantly the friendship and sisterhood. Without them this book wouldn't be possible.

My son Kori Williams, who is my right hand man and always looking out for me. You had to grow up so fast while dealing with your own grief and pain. I know it's hard and sucks even more that your dad is not here, but keep shining and being who you are! Continue to not let your circumstances define you. Your dad is looking down so proud of the young man you have become and striving to be. I love you very much and will always be here for you!

A special thanks to my Mother in Law, Janie Runnels who never left my side and stayed with us in our home for months until I was ready to take on this journey by myself. She helped me through, understood, loved me and supported even when she was dealing with her own grief of losing her son and I wasn't such the greatest person to be around. We had our ups and downs in the process, but it never kept her away. Even when I was being stubborn and isolated that didn't stop her. I call she answer. She kept calling when I wouldn't answer. Her grandson calls she's there. He didn't answer she call again and again. There was a family event or a function that involved her grandson she come to every one of them no matter the missed hours of sleep by working nights as a nurse! It will never be forgotten of the sacrifices you made. We love you with all our heart; you have given us one of the greatest gifts in life.... Your son/his dad! You will always be family to us. Always.

A special shoutout to my nephew; like a second son Marcus Wright. He lived with us for several years and also experienced a lot of pain and grief losing his Uncle Darrell. Marcus was loving, kind, had a huge heart and wanted to see our family unit thrive. He wanted the best for me and his cousin while we put the pieces back together. It will never be forgotten and you will always hold a special place in our heart. We love you.

A special thank you to my one and only sister Shannon Biancamano who was the back bone for my side of the family. My twin, in helping to make sure everything was perfect, organized and helped where she could in the beginning. Even after leaving and being thousands of miles away she was there, supported, cared and did what she could from afar. Most importantly, always keeping Darrell's memory alive and understanding how important that was to us. Sharing stories that we truly believe Darrell came through her to share with me. It will never be forgotten and it was much appreciated. We had special memories with Darrell as a trio and I know you treasure them just as much as I do.

To my friends and family who supported, came running as soon as they heard the news, the numerous people who I knew and to many I didn't know or even remember that came to offer condolences, dropped off meals, watched and entertained my son, household supplies, cleaning services and offered their extended support and much more. To organizations that stepped up to honor and support:

Lewisville Football Association, TRUTH/Deion Sanders Football Organization, Tarheel Basketball Organization, Ozarka Nestle Waters and several city of Lewisville and surrounding communities and businesses. To my church family and to several surrounding church communities that stepped up and were there as well. The ones who understood, prayed, checked in consistently, stuck by my side no matter how much of a monster I was, had patience, were caring and loving through the grieving roller coaster process, and continue to be after all these years.

Thank you to my sister Shannon Biancamano, Ahesha Catalano, and Jennifer Coken who offered their expertise, time and energy to help us bring the book to life. Jennise Beverly, Laneka Jackson, Tanya Howell, Daniella Barbosa, Shannon Perkins, Nyree Jackson were all a part of the process. Thank you for holding the space for us and contributing your time and sharing your journey.

Our readers Minerva Gibbs, Christina Saunders, and Terrance Leftridge (The Unstoppable Coach) we thank you and appreciate you.

Numerous widow friends/groups that I met online and joined through the journey. A lot of them I owe my sanity to.

Maureen

I want to say that my two cherubs Jordan Paige Bobo and Mikayla Quinn Bobo have been the fuel behind the fire of *The Unwelcome Committee*. Early on when I didn't know if up was down or front was back, I looked up and saw their smiling faces and knew I had a purpose. All I knew was that the baby had to be fed, and Jordy had to go to school. No matter what I was going through, those two tasks had to be completed. I believed they were there, yes, as my charge but also to keep me alive. At least that's how I felt at the time. Everything was so very raw, but God knew me and that my mothering instinct would overtake my mood. And here we are, six years later on the road to thriving...But God!

I just want to say a special Thank You to all family and friends who came to the Emergency Room on that tragic day. Especially my sister Sarahita Lee who drove from Euclid, Ohio to Akron, Ohio in, to me, 10 minutes which is usually an hour drive. Also, those who prayed and Loved on me and my children in the aftermath of everything. Your Prayers were truly felt....I LOVE YOU ALL...Be Blessed...MUAH...

I want to give a special dedication to Rebecca Victoria Teague Paige who had aspirations of authoring a book herself...Thank You Ma for your inspiration...I AM REBECCASCHILD...

Khadija

This book is a labor of love! It wouldn't be complete without sharing my utmost gratitude to the two amazing women who persevered through so many storms with me during the process of writing The Unwelcome Committee. Maureen Bobo and Chasity Williams are the definition of conviction, determination, and sisterhood. Thank you for listening, suggesting, cheerleading, and generally having my front, side and back through it all!

To my amazing fantastic five: Latif, Amir, Medina, Qismah, and Sulayman- I love you and want you to know that although your father is no longer here in the physical; he lives through all of you.

Thank you to Ahesha Catalano, Shannon Biancamano and Jennifer Coken who offered their expertise, time and energy to help us bring the book to life. Jennise Beverly, Laneka Jackson, Tanya Howell, Daniella Barbosa, Shannon Perkins, Nyree Jackson were all a part of the process. Thank you for holding the space for us and contributing your time and sharing your journey.

Our readers Minerva Gibbs, Christina Saunders, and Terrance Leftridge (The Unstoppable Coach) we thank you and appreciate you!

A. Karriem Ali, my honey bunny, my love. I will always remember...no matter what...

INTRODUCTION

"For I know the plans I have for you," says the lord. "They are plans for good and not for evil, to give you a future and a hope. In those days when you pray, I will listen. You will find me when you seek me, if you look for me in earnest." "Yes," says the lord, "I will be found by you and I will end your slavery and restore your fortunes, and gather you out of the nations where I sent you and bring you back home again to your own land."
Jeremiah 29:11-14 New Living Translation (NLT)

The above quote was very hard for me to process as a newly widowed woman over nine years ago. And if you are a widow reading this book, you may feel the same. It is my prayer that you will find comfort in the above scripture as I have learned to in these past nine years. I am a firm believer that everything happens for a reason, even the most painful and heartbreaking experiences and events in life. Don't get me wrong; I did not arrive at this revelation instantly. It has taken many days and nights of intense reflection and introspection. I made a conscious choice to look at life differently after going through the many stages of grief. It was an in and out, up and down, roller coaster of a journey. You will get a glimpse of what that was like for me and my widow sisters after reading our stories. You may feel like your life is over, much like I did after getting over the shock of my husband's passing. The truth of the matter is, your life, as you knew it, is over. But I am here to share with you that you can have a new life. A magnificent one. All you have to do is make the choice. Ponder over the above scripture when you feel at the end of your rope.

Meditate on it and decide what it means for you. And as you read this book, know that you are not alone and although you may feel like you are going crazy, you aren't. We are here. Reach out and know you don't have to go it alone.

The introduction is getting the you prepared for what you are about to read, whereas some chapters, like complicated grief, are real and raw. You should be prepared upfront for stuff like that. We don't sugarcoat anything in this book. This is an interactive book. We have included a place for you to reflect on your own journey and thoughts after each chapter. We invite you to journal your feelings and thoughts, as it is important to get it out on paper.

From Maureen

She just didn't know what to do, all in disarray, perturbed, frustrated, angry, depressed, disillusioned, confused, lonely, and any other negative adjective to describe becoming a widow with two children, girls ages eight and two months. Yes, two months! I mean, I understand; that is, we understand. We are the Unwelcome Committee, and we see you. You are not alone on your path of widowhood. This book is a collaboration of three women from different backgrounds but unified for the common cause of welcoming you into your new journey. You don't want to be here, so you are unwelcome. We are so sorry for your loss and share your grief.

We all needed somebody to guide us through the beginning, middle, and many years later stages of this experience. See, you need people all the time because grief never ends; it just changes with time. It knocks you off your axis and completely changes your perspective on life. You are not ready for the challenges being presented to you. They're too much to handle, and we haven't even gotten to the babies yet, have we?

I'm glad you got out of bed today. Maybe you didn't, but that's okay too because you're going through hell. And people may be trying to tell you to hurry up and get out, but if you could get out, you would, wouldn't you? "Grief is a multi-colored avenue. Who knows what color you'll be today?" We want to help guide you through this process through our experiences. It's been very difficult for us, and it will be and already is for you. There is no sugarcoating it. You can't go under, over, or around it. You must go through it, not to be harsh, my little broken friend. We love you (hugs), and we just want to try to help you with support and love. We can relate to what is going on with you, because we have been there. Perhaps you are a friend or relative of someone who has experienced the loss of a spouse at a young age. Maybe reading this book will help you see that person clearer now in the space of their grief, or you can give them this book as a source of comfort. Sometimes just knowing that there are people out there who have been through their path of pain is enough for them to want to see another day. We are the Unwelcome Committee, and we welcome you in.

He comforts us in all our troubles so that we can comfort others. When they are troubled, we will be able to give them the same comfort god has given us.
2 Corinthians 1:4 (NLT)

WHAT HAPPENED

Chasity

Pain changes people.

—Unknown

It was a normal day. I rushed from work to pick up the kids and hurried home to get dinner prepared before Darrell got home. As usual, it being summer time, I knew he would be exhausted from working in the heat all day, so I wanted to make sure dinner was ready for us all when he got there.

He walked in at about 5:45 p.m. and told me quickly that he had just gotten a call from a friend that he saw at the grocery store just a few weeks prior (that he had not seen for years). The friend was excited, as he had gotten a new boat, but he wanted to see if Darrell could come out to help him and look at it, as there was something not right, and they would take it out on the water afterward. Darrell, being who he was and never turning anyone down when they asked for help, decided that he'd run out to the lake really quickly to see what he could do.

I reiterated to him that dinner was almost done and asked if he really needed to go, and he said he would only be an hour, if that. I shrugged it off but wasn't too happy about the decision, and I said, "Alright, whatever." We had a few words back and forth, and he finally left. It wasn't on the greatest terms, but it wasn't bad either. I don't even think I told him a real good-bye.

I remember about an hour after he left, I told myself I would give him another fifteen minutes and then I would try calling him. The boys were getting hungry, so I went ahead and let them eat. About an hour and fifteen minutes went by, and I finally tried calling him, but he did not answer. I kept trying, still no answer. By this point, I was mad and frustrated.

No more than thirty minutes later I received a knock at the door. I looked out the window, and it was the police. The boys were eating dinner at the table, and I remember freaking out and thinking they were there for something that I did: a warrant, something crazy that would have not made any sense. It took me a minute to answer the door, but I finally did. The police officer said "Mrs. Williams, can we speak to you for a minute outside?" At this point, my mind was still racing, and I was wondering what was going on. What they were really there for was the furthest thing from my mind. And within thirty seconds, my whole life changed in an instant when they said, "Mrs. Williams, there has been an accident with your husband."

At this point, I wasn't thinking the worst. I was thinking he was transported to the hospital, he was somewhere where I needed to be, but they told me he had jumped into the water, gone under and they had not seen him since. They said they had rescue crews looking for him. I was in complete shock, and I don't think I really understood the degree of what was happening. I remember rushing into the kids to take them to the neighbor's house so they could be "away" from the news. I did not want them to know what was going on. I made up some absurd story and said that it was nice outside and they could go play with their friends. I had told my neighbors that there had been an accident but not to say anything to the kids at all.

In the meantime, I was in complete panic mode. I was trying to call anyone and everyone that would answer their phone. No one seemed to pick up. I was going in circles. I was running in and out of the house. I was trying to get answers from the cops, but they kept saying the same thing—an answer I didn't want to keep hearing. "Mam, they are searching and will alert us as soon as they find him." I felt helpless, and I wanted to be there. I finally got ahold of a friend that came straight to my house. I wanted to go to the lake right away. I wanted to see with my own eyes what the heck had happened, and talk to his friend to understand what had happened and how.

I do not remember driving to the lake at all, but I remember pulling up to where the boat was docked, and the area was swarmed with news media, ambulances, fire trucks, Lewisville lake wardens, etc. The news media was trying to talk to me, but family members told them to leave me alone. I went up to Darrell's friend and started just rambling off questions. He could not give me any straight answers. He said he too was baffled. He said Darrell had jumped in, and he turned around and Darrell was gone.

I just felt like I wasn't getting any answers. I was scared, emotional, in a daze, and didn't know what to do. I remember more family members showed up, and at this point, I started to break down even more. The paramedics wanted me to sit in their ambulance. At one point they thought that I may need to be transported. All I knew at this point was it was about to be complete darkness and no light, and that meant it would be harder to search for him. Hours went by, darkness appeared, and they told me to return home and that they would begin their search again in the morning. I was in complete denial and did not want this to happen. I instructed them to continue in the dark, no matter what.

They told me there was nothing else I could do. They told me rescue crews were coming to land and that they would keep some people out on the water with sonar equipment and if anything came up, they would inform me ASAP. They said they would continue their search efforts the next day once sunset came. I didn't want to leave the lake, I still wanted answers, I was in denial, and I really thought he was hanging on for dear life somewhere. I knew when I reached home I also had the nightmare of telling the boys, particularly our son, our baby boy, what was going on. I was not ready. I remember I did not sleep, but in reality, I was in such a fog I couldn't tell you what happened during the time period of the four agonizing days of waiting and searching for him.

I remember I had some close friends/coaches by our side when I had to break the news to Kori. I won't ever forget the feeling I had when I had to watch his face and hear him scream out. He was only twelve years old and could not grasp what we had just told him. It was one of the hardest things I will ever do in my life.

I also remember we woke up one morning and went out to the lake with some friends who had a boat. I was at a point where I just didn't think the rescue crew was doing enough. But then again, would anyone really? We had about fifteen to twenty friends/family with us. Some stayed on land, but Kori, some close friends and family, and I got on the boat and the water. I sat at the front of the edge of the boat as Kori sat on the other side of me. We were on the water circling and repeating the routes, screaming his name at the top of our lungs, looking for any sign of him, his clothing, his anything. We did this for about two hours straight, and it came to the time when we knew it was time to dock and we had done all we could.

As we reached the shore, I knew in that exact moment it was real. He was gone. I screamed out, I cried, I yelled, and I cried, until no more tears came down. Friends and family carried me off the boat, as I was too weak to even comprehend in my brain that this was my reality and he was gone. Although he was not found yet, I knew, I just knew. And so did Kori. I didn't even want to go home; I felt like it was just the end.

The day before Father's Day, I woke up, and I didn't really want to talk to or see the visitors that were coming in and out. I was angry, sad, and irritated. How could my life be like this? How? I was cleaning and cleaning and cleaning, people were trying to talk to me, and I was getting upset. I told them to leave me alone, get out of my way; the littlest things were irritating me. I remember getting upset that all the people in and out couldn't have gotten the newspaper in the yard. I ran out to get it, and the first thing I saw was his face on the front page with the big letters, still searching. I came in slammed the door and started vacuuming.

Kori had woken up and was hungry, and not minutes later, a friend came to get Kori to take him to breakfast. I was glad she did, as I was in a mood that was not good for him to be a part of. Ironically, just a few minutes after they left, I saw a woman walking up to the door who I didn't know. I went ahead and went to my room, but my sister came back in to tell me that I needed to come out, as it was the medical examiner.

As soon as I walked in the living room, she explained who she was, and she informed me they had found Darrell. I broke down and did not want to believe her. I started yelling at her that it was not true and she had no proof! "I want proof, lady. Until I see him, I am not going to believe a word you say. It has been four long days; it should not take this long." Then, in that moment, my friend told my sister, "Give it to her, Shannon." She came over and opened up my hand and placed it softly into my hand: his wedding ring. The only thing I could do was cry and cry more. I didn't say another word.

And so it began...

In the early morning hours of June 20, 2009, sleeping restlessly, I became aware of a noise filling the darkness of my bedroom. I listened intently for an accompanying noise. Still on the edge of sleep, I realized the noise in the room was coming from my husband's alarm clock.. Why wasn't he getting up, I wondered. For him to let the alarm go on for so long was unusual, and I started to worry that he would be late for work.

5

Then I remembered. Panic began to rise in my chest. Quickly I calmed myself with the thought that I had surely been dreaming. In this disturbing dream, my husband Darrell was dead. Many family members were at our home. My son had been told, friends had arrived to comfort us, tears had poured out uncontrollably, and somewhere in the back of my mind, I could hear myself screaming. Yes, it must have been a dream. Still, I was afraid to open my eyes. What if he really was dead? Lying there, I imagined that if I stayed very still with eyes squeezed tightly shut, the horror of this dream would fade away with the beginning of the new day.

I slid my hand across to Darrell's side of the bed. To this day, I can still feel the cool, crisp sheet in the place where his warm body should have been. The reality of his absence gripped my heart as the unbelievable memories of the four longs days before came flooding back. Tears flowed again as I repeatedly reached for him, eyes still defiantly closed, wishing desperately to wake up from what was rapidly becoming a nightmare.

That morning I would "officially" begin my first day as a young widow. As time marched on and the initial shock of Darrell's death began to fade, I found being a widow to be both demanding and disconcerting. Not only was I abruptly left without a partner, but I felt the weight of unspoken expectations at every turn. All of a sudden, every decision was mine to make, when I could hardly remember my own name. As my whole being twisted in agony at the thought of life without my husband, the practical pull of daily life continued to demand my attention. Thrust into a fishbowl of well-meaning, sympathetic company, I wavered between the alarming temptation to allow the rising tidal wave of grief to consume me and the equally pressing need to prove that I would not crumble under the weight of despair. The tug-of-war between the desire to fall and the instinct to get up and go was exhausting. Suddenly, my mind was paralyzed by previously inconsequential choices.

Overwhelmed and inexplicably unable to make decisions, I lost the self-confidence on which I had always relied. The moment I lost Darrell, I was transformed from a poised, goal-oriented, content woman into a remote, indecisive, scared monster. I didn't recognize myself, I didn't recognize my life, and I saw no course that would lead me back to the person I used to be. Not only was I lost, but I didn't care that I was lost. Anguish, fear, anxiety, sadness, confusion, and apathy became my constant companions.

Reading about the "stages of grief" frustrates me, because the broad concepts of denial, bargaining, anger, depression, and acceptance are not reflective of my daily experiences. The information I sought about being a widow was more personal. I didn't want to know if other widows had been in denial; I wanted to know if they had worn their husband's clothes. The bargaining phase did not interest me, but I yearned to find out what widows did with their husbands' wedding rings. Being angry about losing your life companion was logical, but where was the logic in believing your dead husband could walk through the door any day?

Depression threatens to consume me daily while hope escapes me. Acceptance is a state I couldn't even consider, so how could I aspire to it? Each time I would enter what I thought was a new stage, I would quickly find myself backtracking and revisiting an old one. Grief begins to seem like an endless maze. I wanted reassurance that I wasn't going to be lost in this labyrinth forever.

It was time to figure out all the planning and funeral arrangements. How do you plan a funeral at thirty-four years old? So many questions and so many whats and hows, and so many people's opinions. This time was such a true fog. But I do remember bits and pieces.

The funeral home is where his body was transferred. I remember walking into that somber, sad place, and the smell of the place was like a hospital or something similar. I was with my mother-in-law, my sister, and a good friend. I remember it just made me sick to my stomach. I was here to plan his funeral, and I was not ready. I still really did not want to believe it. I remember sitting at the round table with the funeral director. The first questioned I asked was when I would get to view Darrell. The director stated, "We are not going to be able to let you see him, Mrs. Williams." At that moment, I went into a rage. They could not tell me what I could do, especially when it came to identifying my husband in person. I wanted and needed to see him. I needed that closure of seeing him with my own eyes. I did not want to take their word. I literally fired questions, my legal rights, and that they could not make that choice for me. This went on for almost two hours, and they finally came to me and said, "Mrs. Williams, if we allow you to see him, we will not allow you to have his services here. We cannot be responsible for your mental state after viewing his body." Then I immediately bawled and sat in silence, as I knew what was really best. They told me with his body being in the water a full four days, I would not even be able to walk in the room due to the smell, and then it would not even look like him. I finally made the decision to not force the viewing of him but to remember him the way I did when he walked out that door for the last time. Some days I wonder if I should have done it, and other days I am glad I did not. I remember walking into the display areas of urns and coffins; this was so eerie and sick feeling. *How do I pick out this?* It came down to no choice. I picked out a beautiful bluish-gray urn that, to us, resembled the Cowboys (yes, the football team). He was a die-hard fan and loved his cowboys. I even purchased a smaller one for his mother to have.

What also sticks out in my memory is my relationship with my mother-in-law. It went from being so close and like she was my mother, to us being like strangers and constantly butting heads. Darrell grew up for eighteen years of his life as a Jehovah's Witness, but his mother did not want to believe he was not practicing any longer. We attended a Christian church, we celebrated birthdays, we celebrated holidays, and the list goes on. Did we respect her still and even visit her church at times? Absolutely! But she did not want to think that we did not practice, especially her son. He never did tell her outright, and that was huge, but it hurt that she did not believe me. It affected a lot of the things we did in preparation for his funeral too.

I look back and wish I would have stood my ground more, but the one most important thing is I knew Darrell would not want us fighting, so I let it be. She stated we could not have his funeral in a church, due to their religious beliefs, even though I could have done it in a church for free because several pastors stepped up to offer me their location. So I went to a funeral home instead to suffice. I paid for every penny of it. Not one offered to help, just gave the stipulations. Then I was told that I could not have any Christian speakers/pastors to recite his funeral. I asked what about me and how I need my peace, and was told if I did that, she would not show up. In my heart, I knew I could not do this. So I respected her. I asked for several friends to get up and speak, and that was where a lot of my peace came from. She had her elder (pastor) get up and speak on Darrell's behalf, and the funeral was so confusing to me, but in the end, it somewhat gave me peace because my friends and family got up and spoke or were there to hold my hand and hug me.

So reality had sunken in, but only some. I didn't want to think it was over. I wanted to think I could still hold on to hope and we would be looking for him. I didn't want this closure. I was not ready to face this reality. His body was officially found floating underneath a popular local restaurant that is on the lake in our city. The medical examiner explained they would transfer his body to where they could examine it and do the normal routine. The results came back, and his first cause of death was proven to be drowning. The second cause of death was listed as a heart attack. They said that is common in drownings, and I am sure he was fighting for his life with every breath he had.

To this day, it is really still a mystery on what actually happened and how he never came back. My theory is he was exhausted from working all day in the heat, hungry, and physically torn down that day, so when he jumped in and maybe got tangled up in something, he could not fight, due to his exhaustion. I have no idea, and that is what hurts even more sometimes. How does a good swimmer, in good shape, who loves water activities, and was a frequent water person, etc., drown? The person he was with claimed he went rushing back to the boat as soon as he heard him "calling" out for help to get the lifesaver, but turned around and was gone. To this day, we are not sure what happened. Results came back, and he had not been drinking, and he was very healthy. I can only wrap my brain around so much before I cannot let it continue to consume me. It was his time, but in the end, I always wonder why so soon.

In the meantime, I was coming up with a plan to tell my son that his father had been found dead. *How do I even fathom telling a twelve-year-old boy his father is gone?* I remember calling in his closet male companions, coaches/friends to be by his side as we told him. It was and will probably be one of the hardest things I will ever have to do in this lifetime. His little mind could not grasp what and why. But even as an adult, I could not either, so how could I expect him to? I remember taking him to his room to sit him down. I was shaking, my heart was beating fast, and I was desperate for anyone to step up and take his pain away and do it for me. I could see it in his eyes; I knew he knew something was about to be shared that would change his life forever. He knew, but as his mother, I had to share, I had to tell him. I remember thinking I could do it later, but it was no turning back, no we will do it later: it was time. I remember my anxiety was so high that I could barely talk, so one of the coaches spoke up and started the dialogue for me. And in that moment, it was done. He busted out in tears and anger at the same time, asking me, "What you mean? They found him didn't they?" He didn't realize he was found dead until I had to say those words: "He is dead, son." I do not remember much after that evening, but know we were surrounded by some close friends at that moment. I am not sure how I would have made it through that without them.

Then our life began, the way we would have never imagined it to be like. Widow. Fatherless. Confused. Angry. Sad. Scared. So many emotions, so many thoughts. What happened changed our lives forever. We were a family of three that changed to a family of two in an instant.

Maureen

Don't be ashamed of your story. It will inspire others.

—Unknown

Well, I don't know how or where to start. What happened, is the question. For me, it is a loaded question. It was so sudden; one minute your husband is dropping you off at work, the next minute you are a widow—I mean, in just a span of a few hours. Martin and I were married for thirteen years and were a making life for ourselves, with our two girls who at the time were ages eight years and two months.

Mine is a story of how health choices affect the entire family and not just the person with the issue. Martin had severe heart disease for ten years. At age thirty-four, he had triple bypass surgery. After his surgery in 1999, the lead surgeon told me that if Martin didn't lose weight, he would be dead in ten years. Martin lived ten and a half years from the surgery. Over the ten-year span, Martin had about six minor heart attacks. In my mind, though, anytime the heart is attacked, it's never minor. Anyway, after each incident, the doctors would say the same thing: make lifestyle changes, exercise, change diet to prolong life. They would prescribe or increase the dosage of the heart medications, and things would go along as normal, or as normal as could be expected.

I look back and realize that Martin had given up before he had started. He had family members who passed away very early of heart-related issues, namely his mother, at age fifty-two. Heart disease was genetic. Having severe heart issues at such a young age, I believe it was

11

overwhelming to Martin. He wanted to live, but I don't think he believed he could. He would say that he knew he would die young, like a self-fulfilling prophecy. Yes, the path to health would be difficult, but half the battle is believing you can do it. Depression sets in; life circumstances, financial, relational, emotional, and spiritual stress closes in on a person, and hope eludes them. I'm sorry to say that this is what happened to my husband.

On April 7, 2010, he succumbed to the chronic heart disease that had plagued him for ten years. I knew before I was told. I called him at work to ask him a question and was told he never made it to work and didn't call. Martin never no-called to work, so something inside me told me that he was gone. He had a heart attack on the way to work, and he hit a parked city street cleaner truck. Fortunately, no one else was hurt. I didn't want to believe it, but I couldn't deny the truth. It was unexpectedly expected. It was like a Mack truck had run over me and then backed up to finish the job. I was in shock. It's hard to explain, but I felt like I was placed in a pitch-black hallway with no way out. The silence of the hallway is enough to drive one insane. When you think about it, the majority of a person's conversation is with their spouse, so when that person suddenly passes away, then life suddenly becomes so quiet it's loud. Meanwhile, I needed to tend to my children; that was my focus. The grief caused me to be afraid that I might die, and then who would raise my children? Early on, the grief waves can overtake you; I felt like I would drown. During this time, you have to have an anchor, and mine is my faith in Christ. He wouldn't let me go, even when at times that was what I wanted. He only gives what we need.

Well, like so many relationships, ours waxed and waned over the years. I believe we loved each other, but neither of us was very good at showing it. I really didn't know what love actually was. I think Martin probably wished that I was more domestic. I grew up with a working mother, so the message that I received was that a woman had to take care of herself, get an education, and go to work. My father worked, but my mother was a teacher and worked the majority of my childhood. When I look back on our marriage, I realize that we didn't discuss the essentials of marriage and how it should run, like who would be in charge of the finances. I wasn't good with the money, and Martin never saw a dollar he didn't want to spend. That attitude spelled disaster in the financial realm of our marriage. It's very difficult to think or even write about. I just tell people that if you can think of anything that could go financially wrong in a family, it happened to the Bobo family. Again, we were young and had our own ideas on things.

What was the purpose of our marriage? I can't answer that, and I don't think Martin could either. Initially, I felt that we communicated well. I was comfortable with sharing the most intimate details of my life with him. Because of our immaturity, neither one of us knew how to handle sensitive topics or be nurturing to each other. A marriage needs to be cultivated daily, or it will not succeed. If the couple is selfish toward one another, then it will fail. Selfishness is what caused our marriage to decline. We didn't know how not to be selfish. I wanted things done my way, he wanted things done his way, and then we were at an impasse. I'll be honest, on many things I did not trust him. He didn't seem to trust me either. We argued often over the last few years of his life.

As the economy turned downward in 2007, so did our relationship. It probably started soon after his heart attack in 1999, but the manifestation of it all came later. We turned from each other, continuing to argue and delving into more financial ruin. The bill collectors were calling, I stopped answering the phone, and Martin began to drink very heavily and stay out all night, coming home in the morning hungover. I felt this was unacceptable, and I told him; he ignored me and continued to drink. He came to me on several occasions and said he had a problem, and I told him that we needed to go to AA, but he wouldn't go. We also needed marriage counseling so we could be reconciled to each other; that didn't happen either. It was having an effect on our daughter because she was acting out in school. She was already active, and I know our arguing and general dislike for each other hurt her more than anything. I guess the message here is marriage is such a fragile thing. People do things in marriage thinking they know best, but it is often to the detriment of the entire family. Then when the husband/wife passes away, all that is left is regret along with severe grief.

I have what they call complicated grief in that I miss Martin but at times I am very angry with him because he didn't take care of himself to prolong his life and he stopped listening to my suggestions to help our family—he let selfishness rule. I get mad at myself because I wasn't mature enough to realize that there is much more to being a wife than what I thought I knew, which wasn't much, if that makes sense. Meanwhile, it's the worst thing to lose a spouse when the relationship is broken.

Living with Heart Disease

Living with a person with heart disease depends on the person who has it. If one is committed to improving their health and living a long, full life, then this will be a challenging yet manageable endeavor. The family would take part in helping their loved one develop the healthy routines needed to prolong their life. All would be well. Unfortunately, this was not the case with Martin. I guess this section could be called the unexpected expected guest or a decade in a heart diseased family.

After Martin had triple bypass surgery in 1999, life went on as normal. Initially, he made some changes, but it didn't take long for the old patterns of unhealthy eating and sedentary lifestyle to come to the forefront. Things were fine until about 2003, when his chest pains started. We had adopted our oldest daughter in March 2002. It was a scary time. Sadly, calling the ambulance became our habit over the next seven years. At least two to four times a year, Martin would have

14

a heart incident requiring hospitalization. Jordan and I spent Thanksgiving 2007 in the hospital with Martin. I am so thankful that Jordan didn't witness me calling the ambulance over the years.

I remember in 2006, after Martin had taken himself to the hospital one night, being told over the phone by the emergency room attending physician that Martin was not going to make it, and I needed to get to the hospital. I had to first take Jordan, age four, to my sister's, an hour away. I got to the hospital, with Martin relaxing in the emergency room in relatively good spirits. Apparently a more experienced cardiologist had examined Martin's vital signs and determined that it was not that serious. To me it was serious; I had driven the hour back from my sister's believing Martin had died. Over that span of time, from 2003–2010, it seemed that Martin had about five to six minor heart attacks, but can a heart attack ever be minor?

I look back today and wonder why we weren't enough for him to make changes. After every ambulance call, I knew this was the end, but it wasn't. Martin started to shut me out. I had worked on my master's degree in social work part time from 2004–2008, and I know this also put a strain on our marriage. Martin wouldn't tell me about his medication or when his doctor's appointments were. He became severely depressed and spoke more and more about dying young. He started drinking and hanging out with friends I didn't even know at bars across Akron. He stopped coming home at night. He started to talk of divorce. We argued constantly. We had lost our son, who came too early in December of 2008. That devastated the both of us. I was pregnant with our daughter. Sex had stopped, and I had to have a procedure called a cerclage so my daughter wouldn't come too early— plus Martin really couldn't anymore. We argued constantly, and our finances were in ruin. The house was about to be foreclosed on, and cars were being repossessed. We were a mess.

Then Martin passed away, but the heart disease didn't. I was left a single parent with a two-month-old and an eight-year-old. I felt so alone and still do sometimes. My now twelve-year-old cries for the father she lost, and my now four-year-old cries for the father she never knew. We remain in recovery from heart disease.

Khadija

The moment may be temporary, but the memory is forever.

—Bud Meyer

I've just begun to scratch the surface of what happened. Karriem, affectionately known as "Ali," passed away on August 13, 2007. He transitioned and took his last breath at 7:28 a.m. that morning. The nurse changed shifts at 7:00 morning, and the woman who came on at that time was warm and pleasant. She knew Ali from a previous hospital stay. Ali had been sweating all night; it was his body's way of shutting down. I held his hand long into the evening and felt his body slowly grow cold. I had sat in a chair beside his bed, sleeping on and off, never letting go of him. I didn't want to let go, because I wanted him to feel that I was there. He'd gone unconscious and wasn't responding. I had read somewhere that your hearing was the last to go, and although I wasn't talking to him, I wanted him to know I was there. The nurse came in to take his vitals and commented on the condition of his hospital gown. She said she couldn't let him lie there in that condition and asked me if it was okay to change his gown. I told her it was okay, but that I would help her, as he had also grown stiff. She proceeded to take off his gown while I held him to one side. When that was done, we turned him over to his other side to continue. And as soon as we were done, we turned him back on his back, and he took one final breath and was gone.

He had gone unconscious Sunday afternoon, and right before he went under, his last words were about a hallucination he'd had about some cats and his father. His best friend, Dawud, and I sat at his bedside chatting about nothing in particular. Not long after he said his last words, one of his coworkers came to see him. Captain Crowe was concerned as he watched Ali lying in the hospital bed. He knew a doctor at Holy Name Hospital and asked her to come take a look at him. She took one look and said he didn't appear to be doing well. She noticed his breathing was very labored. I called in the nurse and asked if she could send the respiratory therapist up to his room. The respiratory therapist came in shortly afterward and assessed his condition, and shook his head. He callously turned up the oxygen to the highest level and then threw up his hand and left the room. I was mortified and hurt that someone could be so cold and nonchalant as my husband lay dying. I jumped up and went to the nurse's station to call Dr. Condemi, Ali's oncologist. When I got him on the phone, I explained what was happening to Ali, from his labored breathing to his unconsciousness. Dr. Condemi was not surprised and informed me that it would not be much longer.

What Happened 2004

I can't remember the exact date and time that we found out he had cancer. But I will always remember the moment the doctor called us into his office, saying he found "something" an pausing to say "it's cancer." I remember us walking out of the office in disbelief; Ali still woozy from the anesthesia. I remember us getting on the elevator and the deafening silence, walking to the car and driving home so he could sleep it off.

I remember the days following the news: getting ready for doctor's appointments (he had to be seen by a surgeon), pre-testing (me yelling at him because he didn't take the barium properly—he was working right up until the night before the surgery and didn't want to be on call at the fire station having to poop), and the day of surgery (him going in and then the waiting).

And finally the surgeon, who had been so optimistic before the surgery, walking slowly down the hall with his head down and a very serious look on his face, coming up to me and his mother and

17

stepfather to explain that he got the mass but that there was more there than he thought. He explained that something told him to take out his liver and check under it, and there he found a few spots of cancer.

And even though that's all he said, somehow I knew that it meant something more serious, and panic crept in.

We asked is we could see him and were led to the post-operation area. There he lay moaning in pain from the incision, semiconscious and eyes closed.

Days later, he would be up and walking around as if he hadn't just had surgery, wanting so bad to get back to doing what he loved most after his family. Weeks later, he was jogging around the park near home and anxiously awaiting the clear from his doctor so he could return to work.

And then chemotherapy began: every other week, on for three days straight. The visiting nurse was herself a colon cancer survivor and would say how well he was doing and how she had beat it but had gone through hell and back. And this went on for six months—every other week, three days straight, hearing the little machine give out doses every fifteen minutes and him losing so much energy, not being able to do anything but sleep. The only "food" he could tolerate was Gatorade.

But on the weeks he didn't have chemo, life was normal: no visiting nurses, no clicking machine, no fatigue. It was as if cancer only invaded our thoughts every other Friday. On Thursdays, we would suddenly get solemn and quiet because we knew what was coming. We knew that our normal life of kids coming and going, school activities, and any other life situations would have to take a backseat once the visiting nurses rolled up to the house

This went on for six months, and the doctors declared him cancer-free, and he went back to doing what he loved. He wasn't completely out of the woods yet. There was still more testing to come, but for now, we could breathe a sigh of relief for at least three months.

Life returned to normal: he started to get accolades for saving people in fires, commendations for bravery involving a horrendous accident on I-95 (an entire family lost, with the exception of their little five-year-old girl).

Fast-forward to December 2006: Noticing him losing weight, asking him if he's going to the doctor, and his mother commenting on his weight loss and asking him if he's going to the doctor. We also decided to separate at this time. We were both going in different directions. He was into his career, and our children were getting older, and I started to question what I wanted to do with my life.

Once Ali was gone, we started to massage his arms and legs to keep him from going into rigor mortis. The funeral director had been called, and Fatimah, my sister-in-law, began making calls. Ali's mother had left a few days before to go home and check on her husband. I began making calls to former neighbors and others. My brother-in-law, Murad, made the funeral arrangements for me, and for that I am grateful. I don't know what state I would have been in to call the funeral director and tell him to come pick up my husband's body. Salaam, my other brother-in-law, pulled out the Holy Quran and began reciting surahs (or chapters) from it. Mona, Ali's first cousin, arrived at the hospital. She came in the room and came over to his body. She asked if she could kiss him, and I told her it was okay. Dawud stood beside Mona, praying over Ali's body. I left the room to go collect myself. My friend Debi never left me alone and came with me. As soon as I got on the elevator, I collapsed in her arms, letting my brave face come off. I went downstairs to eat but still had some phone calls to make. My husband was gone, but I was hungry. What an oxymoron, I thought.

His younger brother Wynton called from Germany to talk to me. I don't remember much about the conversation, but he said he would be on the quickest flight out to be here with the family. With each call I had to make, I got more and more upset. In many instances, I would have to hand Debi the phone to complete the call because I was so distraught. How do you get used to saying to people over and over again that your husband has died? How many more calls would I have to make like this in the coming weeks? How many more calls would I receive where I'd have to relive the experience of watching the father of my children and my life partner, die?

After what felt like a few hours, the funeral director arrived to take Ali's body to the mosque in Paterson. Paterson was the closest Islamic center, and they agreed to hold the janaza (or funeral) there. He entered the hospital room and proceeded to wrap Ali's body up in white sheets. I told him I wanted to ride with them to see where his body would be kept until the janaza the following day. Debi and her partner, Lori, rode with me in Ali's car to the mosque. We drove down Route 4 following behind the tan Chevy Tahoe that held the remains of my husband. The drive was usually a fifteen-minute drive on a normal day, but this day, it seemed to take forever. I kept thinking that this couldn't be real. Why was my husband in the back of an SUV? Were we really following this truck to take his body to the mosque? It felt like I was out of my body, watching the scene in disbelief. I was truly having an out-of-this-world experience.

CHILDREN

Chasity

You never know how strong you are, until being strong is the only choice you have.

—Bob Marley

I think one of the hardest things for me during this widow journey is single parenting and having to make decisions on my own. A spouse is a great bounce board, and a spouse is the only person who has a vested interest in every single decision you make. When you are used to having that for sixteen years of your life and bam, it's gone, you just don't know what to do. When you are faced with making them on your own, you question, am I doing the right thing? You just have to trust your instincts and to go with it. It's extremely difficult and a continual struggle.

I admit I am utterly overwhelmed by having to reinvent myself on so many levels, from the ground up. I don't know where to start, and my fear combines with me just not doing anything. I lack a plan; I don't even know how to make a plan on a course of action. There seems to be too much to do and everything to do, all at the same time. Do I focus more on one specific aspect or goal or try to work on them evenly at the same time? And I have to think of all of this while in the midst of making the right decision and getting my son and nephew on the right track for a successful/happy life.

The bottom line is, there is no one else to share the parenting chores or worry—mainly the worry. That is what will end up eating you alive. Will the boys make the right choices, will they pass their class, will they be safe as they start driving, will I be able to keep them protected and happy on my own? It is a double-edged sword. Not having a partner to rely on forces one to take on more than is probably humanly possible. Knowing that you're the only one out there raising and caring about these kids makes one even more committed to the task.

It is very trying and tiring to be the only one making major decisions for your children and yourself. I have such a fear of making a wrong one. These boys have already gone through way more than most kids their ages will ever encounter. I agonize over my decisions because, in the end, my greatest hope is that these boys will be spared more pain and suffering.

I now worry about my son being able to get into college. What will he study? How will I afford it? What kind of future can I provide him continuing to parent and live on my own? There is no ex-husband to call and say, "We need to meet at the school counselor's office to discuss Kori's bad attitude" or "I need some more help here, please. Can you take the boys an extra weekend so I can have some time to myself? I need to regroup and recharge."

There is such pressure on me to raise these boys to the best of my abilities. But when you can't share some of that responsibility, it wears on you and breaks you down. That is where I'm at right now. No one with whom to mull it over, talk it out, or decide together on the best course of action. Just me. You can rely on people for their opinions and advice, but when it comes down to it, you have to make that ultimate decision, and you are the one that truly has their best interest at heart.

"It takes two to tango." "Two heads are better than one." Yes, I believe all those sayings. I'm so tired and worn out now, I'm not sure how much I can trust myself with those decisions I have to still make.

You care and care and look out for the kids (even bigger ones), and then there is no one to help you. Just a little bit is needed. A hug, being brought dinner, having someone remember to pick up a needed item up from the store. It is like running around on empty all day, every day for weeks, months, years on end. I just have to keep going for a little longer; gas don't run out on me, we're almost there. And more often than not, the gas gauge is on empty! There is always a sense of anxiousness inside me, almost a sense of dread. Running on empty, always trying to be ahead of the game to fend off the potential evil forces.

I have come to know that sometimes everyone needs someone to lean on and rely on. It is a given. Another trait I'm still trying to learn: ask for help.

The point of my ramblings is just that I think all of us have times when we need to lean more rather than having others lean on us. But sometimes it is hard or maybe even impossible to find that.

I have prayed for Darrell to please come to me with some kind of message and advice, but none have come forth. I have begged the universe for guidance and a sense of direction, but again, nothing is speaking to me. No inner or outer voice. Except to hear the sobs of anguish from my sons at times. And I am the only one listening.

I understand sitting here and harping about all of this gets me nowhere. I suppose, in the end, whatever step I end up taking, in whatever direction it is going, is one small step toward the future and going forward and an improvement from stagnating in my current fear and indecision. And in conclusion, God has a plan. I will continue to pray and know that he is in control. I know at times I am asking and praying constantly, but in reality, that is who I need to turn to.

Take a step. Any step. Take a chance, any chance, and see where it leads and what comes of it.

Cast all your anxiety on him because he cares for you.

1 Peter 5:7

Maureen

Out of suffering have emerged the strongest souls.

— *Kahlil Gibran*

Well, the children are a very touchy subject with me. I feel like in this entire process, my children are the ones that are suffering the most. I mean what did they ever do to deserve this? To lose a parent at age eight or at two months. Two ##@@!!! months! Aren't they supposed to have any kind of normalcy in their young lives? What is normalcy anyway? My children are my life. But I often feel like no matter how much I love them, it's never going to be enough. I just cry out to God. What else is there to do? We can't go over, under, or around this issue. One must go through it, and with children, it is very difficult. I really don't know. My eleven-year-old girl, Jordan, cries every Father's Day, and around Christmas time, my three-year-old, Mikayla, cries out for her father, who was snatched from her in infancy. I pray all the time for their protection from all the evils of the world. I'm a social worker, so I know all about the social ills that plague girls from single-parent homes. I can't be caught up in statistics, though, because I really believe that my little family has a much higher calling than some statistic. What that calling is, I'm figuring out as we journey along this path of our grief process. I know it has something to do with helping others. Why would we have to suffer so much pain just for the sake of pain? That makes no sense to me. So there must be more to it, right?

I'm so proud of my girls, though. After they cry, they always get back up and go on with their lives. They never stay and live in their pain. I love that about them. They are better than me in that respect. I can take pain and live there for years. I probably would if it wasn't for my children. I believe the pain of loss has made them more perceptive to others who are hurting, no matter what it is from. Now they are still children, but I see them as highly evolved children, emotionally, if that makes any sense at all. They love on people around them and are not as judgmental. They have joy and peace in their lives. They are my heroes for real. I speak life over them constantly, and I believe they both will do great things in their lives that will help many people. In fact, now that I think about it, I'm more of a problem than they could ever be. They know who they are and where they are going. I worry and get anxious for my girls, but I don't think I should (it's a mom's job to worry anyway); it's going to be all good with them. I pray a battalion of angels with oozies to be encamped around them for protection. I have to silence my mind on the matter. I believe they are going to be just fine.

Children Part 2

Well, I think of my children as both being unexpected blessings. God saw something in my husband, Martin, and me that said, these two people could parent these two children. He definitely saw something in us that we didn't see in ourselves. We would marvel at how beautiful Jordy is and how fortunate we were to be chosen to parent her. You see, Jordy is adopted, and we brought her home from the hospital when she was two days old. Oh, the joy we experienced when the adoption agency called us just three weeks before she was to be born to let us know that we, of all people, had been chosen by the agency to adopt her. Her biological mother wanted the agency to choose who would become her parents. I know it was God's intervention on the matter. Six months prior to that we had an adoption fiasco in which we thought we were going to be able to adopt a child and it didn't work out for us. The disappointment we experienced with that was very painful to bare. But then God.

With Mikayla, we had also experienced a severe tragedy about five months before she was conceived. I was utterly surprised that I found out that I was pregnant when I went for a routine doctor's appointment. I was not overjoyed for some reason. I didn't think I could have children, and immediately, I started to think negatively about the situation. I was scared for the baby; I didn't believe I could carry a baby full term. I basically spoke/thought into my reality because at the next appointment a few weeks later, Martin and I had to rush to the hospital because something was amiss with the baby. I was crushed. I was admitted to the hospital, and they told me that my cervix was not holding and that my water may break. My baby was only eighteen weeks' gestation, and the earliest that a baby could survive was twenty-two weeks. I felt like I was directing a movie. My water did break the next day, and my son did not survive. He was delivered, and Martin and I cried an ocean in that hospital room. I blamed myself for not being more aware of my body and recognizing when things were changing with me. I ignored subtle changes and didn't entertain the idea that I could possibly be pregnant.

I didn't think I could get pregnant. Eight years prior, a doctor told me that I had a bicornuate uterus, so I thought that deformity meant I couldn't get pregnant. He didn't tell me that; I just assumed it, especially after I started doing my own research on the matter. So I figured we would adopt children, and that was that. When I look back on it, we never really tried to get pregnant; it just never happened in like thirteen years of never using any form of birth control. So the more it didn't happen, the more I believed it couldn't happen—what nonsense. This is what happens when a person's thought processes are skewed from the truth. I think that's another book, lol.

Meanwhile, God was at work as usual. After we lost my son, we named him Micah Christian. I was so distraught, I didn't think I would recover. All I could do was cry. I didn't think I would ever get up. After the fog of that loss started to clear, and much prayer, I said to myself, "Well, you see that you can get pregnant and carry a baby pretty far. Why don't you see what you can do?" So we lined up the moon and the stars on everything, and boom bam boom, five months later, Mikayla was conceived. Of course, my negativity immediately kicked in, and I thought she wasn't going to survive, but low and behold she did. Will wonders never cease? After a procedure to strengthen my cervix at about fifteen weeks' gestation, all was good, and she even came one day late. My thoughts couldn't beat out God's blessings, yeah! But alas, it didn't last, because Martin passed away about two months after Mikayla was born, and our life will never be the same.

Khadija

Grief changes the rules, and sometimes rearranges the combinations.

— *Kolleen Ferraco*

My biggest fear became making sure I was physically healthy to be here for my children. I had an unnatural trepidation of not being here for them while they were young and growing. I thought if God would take my husband, who was (in my opinion) the better parent, what would let him keep me here? This is the first time I've brought this up and put it on paper. They say if you fear something, you should run to it and not from it. This is a big deal to me; to even put it down on paper means that I am admitting something so personal. I feel vulnerable exposing my fears. And I'm pretty sure many people feel this way. I know I'm not the only one. But when you have this fear, you feel like you're the only one in the world. And I am the only mother to the "Fantastic Five." No one could possibly replace me.

As they get older and become more independent, I breathe a sigh of relief every time they pass certain milestones. For most of their lives, they have known what it's like to be a part of a family. They know or have known what a two-parent household looks like. The death of their father took away the model of what a family is comprised of.

It was never my desire to be a single mother. Even though there was a point that we contemplated divorce, we still talked about being a family despite our impending divorce. We even sat the children down and told them we were getting a divorce. But we made sure to let them know that Mommy and Daddy still loved each other and were still family. It was never my intention to take my children away from their father. We talked many times about how we would co-parent in our new paradigm.

Six years ago, I could never imagine where I am now: without a male presence in my home for my soon to be thirteen-year-old son, wondering how I teach him to be a young man. I could never imagine having to teach three teenagers how to drive, or lay down the law regarding curfew. I could never imagine having to pay for college, send spending money, fill out financial aid forms, or handle move-in day without my husband. We talked so many nights about their future.

COPING MECHANISMS

Chasity

There's a time to inhale and a time to exhale and a time to just scream it all out!

— Anonymous

Coping with the loss of Darrell has had its extreme ups and downs. I have had several coping mechanisms the last four years, and I am sure as the years go on, the list will grow and change. And it's ironic, as you can see how some of them contradict each other, but the time and the immediate feeling I have at the time is what determines the coping mechanism I tend to use. The following are some of the ways I cope:

- **Having the support of others.** It is important to express your feelings to those close to you and/or who understand. Sometimes sharing your burdens makes them easier to bear. It makes you feel you're not alone or even crazy at times. Joining support groups online, particularly Facebook in my first year is really what got me through, especially when I didn't have too many family members nearby. Meeting others going through the exact thing was just what I needed. Also, when needed, it helps to be able to lean on people that experienced a close personal loss like I did, because I know they will fully understand and "get it."

- **Isolating, gathering my thoughts, rejuvenating, sleeping, and just not talking about it.** It's a "break" from the outside world, having to hear about everyone's "happy" life, etc. I sometimes feel if I just remove myself from everyone and everything, I won't be the burden, or other times I just don't want to talk about any of it. Also, if I know I am in my "funk," I am not going to be the greatest person to be around, so I just separate and isolate.

- **Getting counseling.** I also have had a counselor for four years that I go to on a regular basis. Although my son recently closed, I knew I had still had a lot to work on internally, and I still work through my own grief as a wife. Because as a mother my number one priority was my son and getting him "through" his grief the best possible way that I could, in a sense, it put me on the back burner.

- **Staying busy.** This is one I also use quite often. Keeping things "planned" rather than having to sit in the house was a huge help.

- **Helping others.** I felt if I reached out to others in need, then it would help me feel better about myself—not only in the widow community, but also just overall. I am an active volunteer in a hospice community that I reach out to still. In conclusion, it helps, and it goes along with staying busy. Also, just knowing my insight and background may touch someone else to move forward is worth it all.

- **Talking about him.** I still talk about him, I bring up memories of him, I talk about who he was to my son, I always say "what would Darrell do?" I feel it keeps him alive. Giving a voice to the person he was allows others, especially his son, to do the same. Keeping pictures up, he may be gone, but he is in my sight at all times.

- **Writing.** Just getting my thoughts down on paper is therapeutic and helpful. I also created an "in loving memory" page for him, which helps because I get to see people that still write memories of him or miss just as much.

- **Acknowledging his death and him overall.** I do "angelversaries" for us each year, such as balloon releases, candle vigils, going to the lake where he drowned, cooking his favorite meals, talking about special memories, and writing letters to him. These days tend to turn into more of a "celebration" of his life rather than a sad day. Even though we have sad moments, it helps.

- **Trusting in God and praying.** I have been becoming closer to God, going to church, reading the Bible, praying, and surrounding myself with like-minded people, as such has helped me tremendously. I recently started opening my house up every Wednesday night for Bible study and have a mentor that is allowing me to learn more about the Bible and dwelling in Christ, which I didn't learn growing up. Growing more in this area has helped me tremendously. Most importantly, knowing I will be getting to see him again brings so much joy and peace.

- **Eating/enjoying food.** As strange as it may sound, and though it may not be the greatest, one of my ways of coping was to eat/be comforted by food. When I was bored, sad, or even alone, I would turn to sweets and food. I still do at times.

- **Listening to songs/music.** I think this is self-explanatory, but sometimes just dwelling on songs of loss or even songs that remind me of him or that were "our songs," brought a sense of peace and sense he was near.

- **Reading inspirational/self-development/spiritual books.** My "library" definitely grew through this time. I like to read, and books that can help. My collection still growing.

- **Connecting through social media.** Through social media, I was able to join widow groups and connect with other widows, making lifetime connections.

Maureen

When you come out of the storm you won't be the same person that walked in . . . That's what the storm is all about.

—Haruki Murakami

In psychology, *coping* is expending conscious effort to solve personal and interpersonal problems, and seeking to master, minimize, or tolerate stress or conflict. Well, with all that being said, I believe when one becomes a widow, all bets are off. I mean, you are so thrown off then; how do you possibly cope? I think sometimes you just have to breathe in and out. And frankly, sometimes you can't even do that.

When I first became a widow in April 2010, I didn't realize the journey that I am currently on would change me forever. Suddenly becoming a single parent was the most frightening thing that could ever happen. Where I was once Mom, I became Mom and Dad in an instant. At least at that time that was what I felt like. Now I realize that I could never be Dad: he fulfilled within the children a need that I could never fill. It took me a year to realize that. When grief hits, the thought process sometimes goes out the window and takes a while to come back to earth, if it ever does.

As time went on and I think of how I coped, I was coping whether I knew it or not, because everyone copes in some way, whether healthy or not. I hid my feelings and continued to feel isolated. I just thought that no one wanted to deal with the heaviness of what I was and still am dealing with. I still feel that way, and I don't think anything will change that. I just don't like to burden people and bring them down. Plus, I know they could never understand unless they have walked in my shoes. So therein lies the problem. I don't want people in my support system to ever have to walk in my shoes and understand my pain. So they can't help me. They can smile and be nice, but ultimately, only those who know the real deal of this matter can help.

I remember now that I did sleep a lot. I know I did this to go to another reality so that I didn't have to live in my reality. It's sad but true. My reality was a very dark, very lonely hallway in which I sensed others were there, but I knew that I felt alone. I felt hopeless, as if I would never get out. I had thoughts of death and wondered if God wanted me to die, too. I was afraid for my children. It was the initial what I call the "going through process." It's when the grief waves are the fiercest and you are trying to hold on for dear life to the anchor that you have. My anchor was and still is God. I felt that I was going to drown, and he was making me a very seasoned sailor with those waves.

I did go under after about a year. I had what I believe was major depression for the majority of 2011. Most people who knew wouldn't believe it I bet, because I am very good at putting on a front. I was dying inside. I didn't feel anyone would ever love me, and I felt so sorry for my children to have me as a mom, an always tired, good-for-nothing, SMH. See I had a serious self-worth issue, and this entire grief process magnifies all issues you may have. I had nothing good to say about me. It was to a point that I started to realize that my response to anything about my life, circumstances, future, or anything had a negative tone. That is very not good, SMH. Positivity was a foreign word to me. I guess I had literally decades of self-hatred ideology to work through before I could get to a point where I could turn toward the positive.

I read somewhere that the absence of unconditional love is the basis of low self-esteem. That hit the nail on the head. I wasn't loved unconditionally by my father. He did his duty and was a great provider, but I always thought he didn't like me, so I took into my life that thought that people just didn't like me. It affected how I went about doing basically everything in my life. So first, for me to even try to cope effectively, I had to examine myself. In doing that, I realized that I needed love. Not just any love, but love of me, self-love, bingo!

For me, coping started with Maureen loving Maureen. Nothing in my life would ever move forward until that happened.

Now that I feel like I have the key to the treasure. I'm on a journey of self-discovery of how great I am. It's awesome. I'm not saying everything is wonderful and I am done grieving. I'm not sure that grief ever ends, but one thing is for sure: if you have to be with yourself anyway, then you might as well love the one you're with, as they say. Stay tuned. :)

Khadija

I believe the first year I spent pretending so much that shock was a part of coping with Ali's death. I used to pretend that he was doing overtime or that he was away on a fishing trip with his platoon. And even though I attended counseling and even went to a psychiatrist for medication, I still was in shock, and I don't think the psychiatrist or counselor understood what I was really dealing with. My symptoms were manifesting grief. I would have panic attacks, dizzy spells, and migraine headaches. I went to doctors, emergency rooms, neurologists—you name it! And all it was, in my opinion, was grief. Grief was manifesting in physical symptoms because I wouldn't talk about how I was feeling (I had no one with whom to express how I really felt and was dealing with complicated grief).

The next phase after the year wore out was raw pain. The realization that he was not coming back finally hit me after the year was up. I turned to alcohol and drugs to cope. I tried drinking and smoking my pain away. Marijuana proved very quickly to not be the solution because I would have panic attacks every time I smoked. After one particular episode where I hallucinated and thought I was dying, I gave up smoking for good. But alcohol was still on my radar. It felt fun and made me feel free and happy. But if I was honest with myself, after the high was over, I was still left to deal with my feelings of grief.

BALANCE

Chasity

Life is a balance of holding on and letting go.

—Rumi

"Balance? What is that?" I say on some or even most days. Before I lost Darrell, I was very in tune with our surroundings. I knew what needed to be done/where to be, our tedious schedules, our appointments, and anything else we could squeeze in. I was on top of it; I was the one who made sure it all "happened." And I worked a forty plus hour work week! I was organized, I remembered everything and had tons of energy. Oh, did I mention I was on time for everything! I even left early to arrive early. I was superwoman and proud of it.

Now, I forget; my mind wanders; I overthink things; I constantly try to keep up and find out I can't keep up with everything. I am typically on time on the dot, which is late for me, or I am late! Oh, did I mention I am drained in the whole process? All the calendars and tools in the world couldn't help my poor soul either. At the same time, I am trying to follow through and do what is needed, without slipping and feeling guilty about it. This is not my personality; this is not who I am. It bugs me to no end that sometimes the simplicity of things can cause so much chaos and havoc. Some people would think I can control all of this, but in the end, when you are used to having another person/parent to help you day in and day out, it's a huge adjustment that may take years to get used to, if you ever do! I also have never been solo. I went from my parents' house at seventeen to live with Darrell's cousin Robin, then at twenty moved in with Darrell. So just living alone was another huge adjustment in itself.

Balancing my career and child raising in the years alone has been one of the hardest tasks in my life so far, I think. It's not so much the practical issue of finding help; it's the need to support my son and nephew through their grief while coping with mine, on top of raising them to be good people and making sure they have the best possible life and become the best adults I can set them up to be. Not to mention the tremendous anxiety stemming from knowing that 100 percent of the responsibility for them is resting on my shoulders alone.

A balanced life is not easy for widows. Not only is our partner gone, but also the finances may be more limited or burdensome to handle, which causes stress to your balance. And other relationships may be shifting. While some friends and family may become closer than ever and new friends may appear, some may fade away. Friends of the couple may not remain friends of the widow, and in-laws may not remain close. This can cause you to need to ask for help or to know whom you can rely on, etc. The challenge during this time of change is to regain a degree of balance in the context of a new life, as well.

The bottom line is, I used to have help. I could lean on Darrell to help cook, clean, attend school meetings. We'd switch off, and he'd do things so I could stay home and be productive or just take some "me time." The little things really helped. There are so many things that I could add to this list, but driving solo sucks, and it's hard. I don't care how many tools you can have in place, it will still be hard.

Learning to say no to certain things, putting yourself as a priority, asking for help, creating me time, making lists, taking time out, and so on, is so much easier said than done. Point blank, there are just some things you would not ask of others, or maybe you don't want them to partake in or know that part of your life. Or they can't do it, such as private things like parent-teacher conferences, counseling, etc., or they can't go work your job for you for a day or two. And in the end, we know if you do something yourself, the outcome is more likely to be what you are looking for. I am getting better in this area but still have a long way to go!

One thing that I recall reading is something that I need to remind myself of daily:

When everything in our world keeps changing, we get confused about how to keep the main thing the main thing. It may even be difficult to determine what the main thing ought to be. And that's why it's important we choose to focus on those things that never change. As far as I know, it's a very short list: (1) God, and (2) his word. If I let my focus wander from those, life can get blurry in a hurry.

— unknown

Maureen

I always saw the light at the end of the tunnels. Sometimes it was really dim, but it never went out. Now it shines bright. I feel its warmth on my cheeks, and I start smiling.

— Maureen Bobo

Hmmm, balance, what to say, what to say. I guess when I think of the balancing acts that go along with being a widow with children, I think of an elephant on a see-saw with a mouse; there is just no balance there. I am overwhelmed on all fronts. Where there were once two people caring for two children, it became one person (and sometimes I'm so tired, I feel like three-fourths of a person) caring for two people. Then, in my estimation, each child needs two individual parents, so that's really four parents and I'm only one person. That's my single parent math for basically that's how tired I am a lot of the time.

I was always an independent-type person, so I didn't know anything about asking for help on things like picking up my children or just taking them for a few hours while I take care of things (that's code for take a nap, and by a few hours, I mean all day). I guess I'm still not comfortable with asking for help, even from my own family. I never want to impose. It's a faulty thought process on my part, I know, because as a Christian, we are taught that we are all dependent on each other as one body in Christ. Well, the Lord is still working on me in this area. I'm getting better, but I know I have a ways to go. It may be that I don't want to be judged because I don't have it all together with things. How could I, when I am a one-legged marathon runner in life. I believe God is the spiritual other leg helping along this widow's with children walk. Where I am weak (which is a lot of places), he is definitely strong. But who wants to be weak? Nobody, but that is where the glory of God is, or in secular terms, the magic is happening in the weak spots or outside the box. I notice that many times things are getting done, and I really don't know how it is happening.

I often feel sorry for my children in the aspect of balance because I feel like they are missing out on sooo much. I mean fathers matter a lot. A child needs to have a male perspective on life, plus, to me, children need to see examples of a loving couple in their life. How are they to learn to be in a loving relationship with their spouses if they don't see this? See, I have questions and expectations for God. Me and him are having ongoing conversations about this and other things. He's working on me and knows I have issues with the way things have gone for my children. I'll just be honest; he knows I am angry with him sometimes about my children being somewhat amputated in the parenting arena. I'm like, "God, you know I'm just a tired so and so. You mean to tell me that I'm supposed to be able to parent them by myself?" (I say that a lot, so much so that my older daughter, Jordan, commented on it.) Anyway, he says, "You've been doing it, and I am God. Remember I got this and you, child of mine. He's so patient with me and loving; his grace is sufficient, especially when I'm throwing a tantrum about our life and crying out to him on his plans for us and how I don't see things he's telling me (vision). I get back; just be faithful, watch and see.

Meanwhile, I'm so proud of my two cherubs, girls ages three and eleven. They are the greatest show on earth to me: so well-adjusted, kind, loving, and just plain old good people. I'm still trying to figure out where they both came from. My older girl, Jordy, misses her dad, and I feel for her. A child should have an out when they can't get their way with one parent; it's just not fair. Momma's rule is law, so what does a child do but cry? My younger girl, Mikayla, has no idea what having a father is, and she asks about him and cries for him. She misses him. She's not sure what she's missing, but she's smart enough to know something is not there, and it breaks my heart for them both. You see, that is why I'm like, "God, what are you doing in this instance for my babies? Forget me; I don't matter, but the babies, Lord" (at this point I'm in tears). He just says, "Trust me," so I do.

Khadija

Balance...

Ha! In the first year of widowhood, I was still in a fog and couldn't even imagine what balance meant. I spent so many weeks settling his estate and sending thank you notes that I didn't have time to stop and think about balance. My first taste of what was to come occurred on a day I couldn't pick up my youngest son from aftercare. I called Ali's closest friend to ask him to get my son. He did and quickly brought him to me. I was a little taken back at the hastiness of him to drop my son off. Nevertheless, I didn't say anything about it and kept on moving.

I discovered very early on I would be on my own, that people only shared empty words and promises and that I would ultimately be responsible for these five souls on my own. There were many times I could use help with raising them. My oldest two gave me a run for my

39

money very early on after their father passed away (one word: rebellion), and in the end, I called on family to help, and one family member enabled my daughter in her rebellion! These experiences left me with a lot of bitterness and anger. Anger because why did my husband leave me to handle this big responsibility alone? Bitterness because people who told me they'd be there suddenly went back to their own lives, not worrying or caring about what I had on my plate with five children.

But what I've learned through all of this is self-reliance. I've learned that God calls his strongest, and I needed to learn that people are people and they talk. They give empty promises to make themselves feel better. I've learned that God always takes care of his own. There have been many times I knew God was in the midst of the situation and I was just too blinded by anger and bitterness to see. Nowadays, when I'm hit with a conflict of scheduling, I just ask, "How can I make this work?" Sometimes, I ask God to send someone who will help me. Other times, I simply surrender and don't give in to despair. Recently, my son started playing baseball, and some nights his games are on nights where I have my business meetings. Me missing my meeting is non-negotiable and also it is important for my son to be involved in an activity (he has ADHD and is on the autism spectrum). Since getting involved with developing myself personally, spiritually, and emotionally, I've learned that successful people think "both," while unsuccessful people think "either/or." So instead of me reacting to the fact that I have a conflict, I now think, "How can I make this work?" So I started taking the metro to my meetings and letting my daughter drive my son to the games. It has become a matter of trusting my daughter with the car, confronting my fear of change (riding the metro in DC is no laughing matter), and sometimes getting in a conflict with the coach about why my son is late. I've been able to handle all of these situations, not letting my fear get the best of me!

In truth, being a single mom, there will never be true balance. After all, you are missing the other half of the equation. What I've learned to do is to ask myself better quality questions, and trust that God has the rest.

Balance in Parenting

The balance our family was compromised. Seven years later, it still is. The other half of the energy needed to have balance in our family is no longer here. No matter how hard I try, I can never be a father to my children. I can only be their mother. In the beginning, right after his death, boy I sure did try to throw my weight around with masculine energy. I would tussle with my oldest son. We encountered many tugs-of-war. We laugh about it now, but looking back, I honestly did not know how to relate to my son, who was right on the cusp of becoming a young man when his father died. In reality, I did not even know how to raise two teenage girls without a male presence. There were times when their father could say a few words to help them understand. He had a tenderness and understanding spirit with our children that I did not possess. He could talk and reason with them in a way I couldn't.

After his death, my relationship with my son and daughters suffered greatly. Their father was no longer there as a buffer. I had to learn to speak to them with reason, whereas before, I always had his word to back me up with discipline or rules. My youngest son, who was only six when his father died, didn't get to experience being around Ali to learn how to be a man. To this day, I worry about him having enough male influences in his life. All the friends my husband had before he died are no longer around. All the promises to come and get my youngest son to make sure he had that influence died with my husband. At first, I was so angry at his friends for what I felt was abandonment. But now, I just chalk it up to life. I pray that I am doing the best I can as a mother.

41

ISOLATION

Chasity

When you find yourself cocooned in isolation and despair and cannot find your way out of the darkness, remember that this is similar to the place where caterpillars go to grow their wings.

—Unknown

What does the word the *isolation* mean? According to the Collins English Dictionary, it means in sociology, "a lack of contact between persons, groups, or whole societies," and in social psychology, "the failure of an individual to maintain contact with others or genuine communication where interaction with others persists."

Yes, that was me a lot of times through this grief journey and even at times now. I felt like isolation was sometimes the best remedy rather than having to deal with issues at hand. I felt if I didn't interact with people, I could avoid the questions, the statements of sympathy, and even the invites to do something. Isolation kept me from realizing my reality at times too. People trying to make small talk and not knowing exactly what to say, telling me about their life, etc., just made my reality maximize, as I wanted, needed my husband more than ever. I didn't want to hear their stories, their little complaints, or even about their extravagant adventure with the family. It was hard for me to hear things of this nature because it reminded me that my husband was no longer here. It wasn't fair.

A lot of times it was very hard to have the energy to associate with others. And I felt I had to be someone that I was not. I basically felt I was going to be pressured to talk about things and had to put on this strong image that I was doing okay, when really, inside, I was suffering and sad. When you're widowed at a young age, there aren't that many other people out there walking in your shoes. It became very frustrating to try to explain the extreme impact of my husband's death to others. Or even justify my actions and/or reasoning for why I was acting a certain way on a certain day, when yesterday I was "okay."

It just always felt as though I was talking to brick wall. People would give words of sympathy, and even said they understood, but I could tell they didn't really fully comprehend the depth of my pain. Oftentimes, I'd hear criticism about what I was doing, how I was doing it, or what I should be doing, and was told that whatever it was I was being criticized for always seemed to increase my grief. I felt criticized for grieving or not grieving right. At times I even felt that I wasn't upholding my relationships with close friends and family the way I should be, so I started to second-guess myself. Sometimes I thought I was going crazy,

Immediately after Darrell's death, we received an overwhelming wave of support and attention. Then, it was like entering a desert of isolation, or dropping off a cliff where the excruciating memories haunted me. Suddenly, I was expected to move on with our life: continue business as usual it was x amount of months, I should be better or not act so selfishly. But what people don't understand is that about the time the shock wears off, the numbness that has comforted us has gone away, and the raw reality of his death is here to deal with. Just me. Alone. Others do not have to deal with the reality; they miss him and maybe even long to hear his voice again, but they don't have to deal with the everyday things that he would have brought to his immediate family and me.

Another side of isolation for me is that I feel I can "deal" with my feelings by evaluating what is going on within. I sometimes start analyzing the reason I isolate. Taking a "break" from people, things helps. Some people view that as being rude. Maybe there is a bigger picture here, but I still to this day tend to isolate.

Also, Darrell always tended to be the more outgoing, social, super nice guy that got along with everyone. He was so laid back as I tended to be skeptical, analyze people, and observe. So in a way, we balanced each other out. He made me feel comfortable in social settings. So in a way, isolation kept me from feeling uncomfortable, not knowing how to act, etc. It is harder for me to build relationships, though it came naturally for Darrell. And maybe as the years went on, isolation was the key to me to not get hurt or have my expectations broken.

In the end, if I don't isolate myself to get through the fight, I won't last long. That's not choosing isolation; it's for survival. I take myself out of the loop of people/things, and it helps me reevaluate and get back on track. Is that right and/or okay? Some would probably debate it.

Maureen

After being broken into one thousand pieces, I realized only God's love could heal me one piece at a time.

—Maureen Bobo

My isolation after Martin's death was, to me, a continuation of my life's isolation. See, I was what I've coined an "islolationist," meaning I was already the type of person who shied away from people. This was something rooted in me from childhood. I realize now that I did this because I believed people didn't like me anyway, so I would push them away first to save myself some pain. It was a stronghold that I'm just now being able to pull down. I wasn't a cute little skinny girl. No, I was chubby, ugly Maureen (my perception of me), so who wants to be around her? That's how I lived my life. I regret the choices I made with this as the foundation of my perspective on my life. How many great people did I push away, not even giving them a chance to come into my life? This perspective dictated my choices. Most of the time, I was alone and lonely, even in my marriage. I really don't even know how I was able to get married. God, I guess.

Anyway, after Martin's death, I went on childcare mode. I didn't want to see or hear anything because "my babies" had been traumatized and they needed me to protect them. I was going to be their savior. No one else was going to be able to help us. I became good at pretending everything was alright. I was already pretending in my life, so it wasn't that much of a stretch to pretend even more. I guess I didn't want to make people more uncomfortable around me and my situation, so I stayed out of people's way. I went back to work too soon, trying to make my life like it used to be. I had to learn the hard way that you can never go home again. I hated my life and myself and was soooo very lonely. I hurt every day, blamed myself for killing Martin, and wept for my poor children for having me as a mother.

In 2011, after being fired from a job I shouldn't have been on, I had what I call a breakdown. It all crashed: the loneliness was getting to me, no one understood me, I had no one to talk to, no one to relate to, I wanted to go to sleep and never wake up—not kill myself, just sleep forever. I felt my brokenness, I was shattered, I was useless, I had no voice because there were not ears to hear me. Again, instead of me saving my children, they saved me. I'm not really sure what my next move would have been without them, but with them, I picked up the phone to get some help for us, for me. I got into a grief group that started me on the ongoing journey to process my grief and isolation. I was not alone anymore. I realized I never really was.

Khadija

It's not the load that breaks you down, it's the way you carry it.

— Lena Horne

Isolation began a few weeks after Ali died. My expectations of people died after a few incidents that spanned several years after he passed away. The phone calls, people promising to keep in contact, and offers of sympathy and concern went away. People went back to their perfect lives, and I was left alone to deal with my children and my emotions. I hadn't had any time to process what happened as it was. Before his death, I had been preoccupied with visiting him in the hospital daily, keeping up with the kids' movements, making sure we had food, shelter, and money to gas up our cars. His prescriptions alone were costing anywhere from $500 plus a month. We were living with my stepfather. Eight people in a two-bedroom home.

I kept my emotions to myself because I had to put on a face of bravery, for my children and for my husband. I was being pulled in so many directions, and I felt like an old Raggedy Ann doll. I had so many holes and strings missing that the least bit of friction might cause me to come apart. The situation, like a train, had to keep moving. There was no space for falling apart and coming loose at the seams. I bottled up my emotions a lot during his illness. And I would find out after he was gone how detrimental that was to me.

Much of my isolation happened after finding out that people weren't as supportive as they said they would be. There were also those people that avoided me when at community functions. Another firefighter died tragically in a motorcycle accident after Ali passed away. The children and I attended the function, only to be shunned and avoided while there. I was shocked and hurt. Ali had had colon cancer and died, and now it felt like I had some kind of disease to be avoided at all cost. It was disheartening to me to find the people I thought I could depend on, avoiding me and going back on their word. It was betrayal in my mind. I became very depressed, angry, and sad.

I shopped to dull the pain and spent thousands of dollars unnecessarily. I overate and gained fifty pounds. The shopping made me feel better for a fraction of a minute, and I would be back in the same rut less than forty-eight hours later. The food only made me feel good while I was eating it. The moment I would finish eating, my mood would turn sour and sullen. I snapped and yelled at my children constantly. In short, I was a mess! No one could understand what I was feeling. No one could relate. I found a young widow/widowers website online and would spend hours perusing the website, until the wee hours of the morning. I couldn't talk to the friends I had left because they just didn't understand the level at which I was grieving. Some tried to be there for me as best they could. And many times I shut people out. I couldn't express my utter sadness that Ali and I didn't get the time to really reconcile our relationship. I couldn't put into words the feeling I had walking around in a fog, or looking at people wondering why they even bothered to live knowing they would die someday.

People didn't want to hear my pain. They wanted to continue their lives as they knew them. I however, couldn't continue as I knew it. My spouse, my lover, my protector, the father of my babies was gone— forever. I would have vivid dreams of him coming out of the grave, still shrouded in his white garments. I'd be so happy to see him. In the dream, I would remember feeling such relief that he was indeed still with us. But then I'd wake up feeling like reality was the dream, that it was all backward, that the dream was what was real. I ached in my heart realizing this new paradigm in my life and in my children's lives.

BEING SINGLE

Chasity

Stop waiting for love and start living. There are many stories your life is meant to tell. Finding love is just one chapter.

—Mandy Hale

Being single, where do I start? I could write forever on this topic, and in so many different aspects.

As the years have gone by, I have become more at peace with Darrell's death and him not being here, but realistically, I miss his companionship and friendship the most. I miss his presence to tell him things, good or bad; I miss his touch, the warmth of his body next to mine; I miss the feeling of security and sense of protection. I miss just hanging out. I miss not having someone to immediately lean on for bad days, advice, or just being there. I miss not being able to just pick up the phone and call him about things that he would be happy for me/us about. I miss the person who knew me the best. I miss when everyone else in the outside world is being fake, rude, or unreal, that he would still be there and those others wouldn't matter.

You lose your second half and have the struggle of trying to find out who you are as a person (not a wife) and getting used to stepping up, scared or not, because you have no choice. It sucks to hear about others' relationships. Being the third wheel or sometimes the fourth, fifth, or sixth wheel makes you think about the what-ifs and the future you will never get to fulfill. I wonder how it would have been and how things would be different. But, with all that, I do sometimes wonder if we would still be together. I wonder if I would be the person I am now, the one I evolved into as I aged. I wonder if he would like who I have become. I wonder about things and if he did this or that, and some things I will never have answers for.

Now for the flipside of being single and the "single life." I have always been a very independent person, not asking for help, doing my own things my way, so having to depend on another man is not needed or a priority. I can definitely say I am set in my ways; I know what I want and what I don't and won't deal with. I think a strong, independent woman who is doing well for herself threatens men. One thing I deal with a lot is married men and their advances. I stay full clear of these boys (yes boys), as how the heck do they think I'm going to hook up with them? Then if they are not married, all they want to do is have sex, not be committed. I was with Darrell for sixteen years, since I was eighteen, and I definitely see relationships at a different, mature level.

A hurtful thing during this process is also my married friends dropping off, due to the wife feeling threatened and their insecurities getting in the way. I have to remember it really doesn't have anything to do with me, but it hurts to think they think I would ruin their marriage. I am a better person than that. I would never do that to someone's marriage, let alone a friend of mine.

Sometimes I feel like I am ready to date, other times not. I am not sure I have the time to invest into a relationship since I have the boys to care for right now, but others would say I need to make time. I am scared to see what it may offer. I always hear I have to get out there to see what may come to me. The flipside of this is my son, Kori. He is not ready, but when will he ever be? I always say that when he experiences his first love, he will understand what it means and feels like. Right now, he sees other men as a replacement for his dad. And on a deeper level, he thinks we won't meet again in heaven if I marry someone else. I think as he matures more, this will subside.

Another side to this is I feel being single gives me time to work on me, finding out who I am as a person, not a wife or a mom. Finding my purpose, living the life I want happily. Having the determination to be the best woman I can be. Fixing flaws, enhancing myself, learning and loving better. Knowing that I won't just settle.

Maureen

Love when you're ready, not when you're lonely.

—Unknown

I guess singleness can be defined in many different terms, depending on your perspective. I am single, but how am I single? I am not married, yes, but how do I choose to live in my singleness?

I didn't really recognize my being single until a year after Martin passed away. I mean, I knew I was alone, raising two children. I was always tired, didn't want to get out of bed, only looking forward to more nothingness in my life, alone and lonely. I hadn't labeled it yet, but I felt it big time. How does that realization actually feel? Loneliness is being in a dark hallway with no way out, but being alone is in the same hallway but with exits all around. It's a choice; I call it solitude, alone with peace.

It took me three and a half years to get to my solitude spot. I had to be locked in that dark hallway with me to like it there, see. I didn't like me and wanted to get away from me. I was having thoughts of meeting someone when I was sixty-eight! Like why sixty-eight? Who knows, just a number far, far away to make me feel more alone. Anyway, while crying out to God at my situation—not only am I a single parent, but also my children will never have a father, a black loving couple every day; i'll spend the rest of my days without a snuggle partner, humble berry love muffin; no hand to hold, lips to kiss, receiving entry from no one; miserable am I—I wanted someone, anyone to see me and make me feel alive. I think God was like, "You need a lot of work . . ." And I did.

I realize now that I wasn't fit to be in a relationship, as long as I wanted to fulfill myself outside of myself. Men looked at me, spoke to me, but nothing else. I wondered what was wrong with me. I started observing men, listening to men and topics on men, and at the same time, I started working on me. This was 2011. What I discovered about men was that they have to pursue a woman. If they want her, then they will. If they don't, they won't. There's nothing she can do about it; one can't force it. But what I've also found in my observations is that women are willing to do anything to get a man, so men actually don't have to pursue, because they are constantly being pursued by women. No matter where a man is in life, there is usually some woman willing to be with him. That's a problem. Women devalue themselves trying to find happiness in just having a man, who may not even want them, just what they are willing to give (a lot of sex!).

I follow Christ and am celibate. I don't go around screaming that out, but I want God's purposes in my life. I believe in my faith walk with God as I fulfill his purposes. I will come in contact with the God-ordained key bearer to my heart (I know it's a bit much, lol, but it's how I feel on the matter). We will come together to glorify God in our marriage and fulfill our destiny together.

Meanwhile, over the course of the three and a half years of my self-discovery in my singleness, I've learned to love me, finally! It took long enough. God's probably like "By George, I think she's got it!" (In a British accent, lol.) It's the key to everything! One's life doesn't begin until they love themselves, until they don't want to please anyone but God, not people. Also, I'm free! Chains are broken! I'm a woman on fiyah! I heard someone say that a woman who has high self-esteem inoculates her daughters from their own self-hatred. That right there is worth any struggles I may face in my single life.

51

Khadija

Don't look for someone who will solve all your problems. Look for someone who won't let you face them alone.

—Unknown

It's been six years since Ali passed. At one point, I was so busy with the kids that I didn't think about dating initially. But then panic set in when I realized I might never have sex again—just keeping it real. Ali and I never had problems in the bedroom. When he passed, I was in my sexual prime. I had so many fears, thinking back at that time. I had a fear of being alone, fear of being by myself, fear of never loving again. All of this tied into my identity at the time. I didn't know who I was. I had always been his wife and the mother of my children. I had no identity. We had married so early and began our family immediately. I had had no time to think about who Khadija was.

Years later, I stumbled and fell and started to question what was going on around me. I don't think I identified with it as "finding myself." I was so unaware consciously. I had let so many outside influences define who I was. Everything was everyone else's fault but mine. I was truly ignorant. Not necessarily in behavior, I just did not have any direction or purpose outside of being a mom and a wife. There's quite a bit I am leaving out in my journey here, but let's just say I made a lot of mistakes (that stemmed from low self-esteem in childhood).

Fast-forward to him passing away, I contemplated what to do now as a single woman and a single mom. Back then, the thought of being called a single mom made my skin crawl. A single mom who was, in turn, raised by her single mom, had raised me. I had beaten the odds by marrying my high school sweetheart and raising my children in a family unit. Now that he was gone, I was put into a category I had so desperately fought to stay out of. I had been breaking the family curse of single parenthood (or so I thought).

My first real relationship came in 2010, right before I moved to Maryland. He was an old family friend, someone I'd known for over twenty years. We started off driving to see his sister and found we got along. I saw a different side to him that I had not previously paid attention to. He made me laugh, which was something I hadn't done in a long time. My feelings grew for him, and even though I knew I had to move for what I thought was a better life for me and the kids, it was hard leaving a piece of my heart behind in New Jersey. I was in love (or so I thought) for the first time since Ali had passed. One of the many reasons I loved him was because even though I was still grieving for Ali, I was able to talk to him about my sorrow and sadness. I was still going through waves of grief, and he would always lend a sympathetic ear.

We kept our relationship going for two years. It ended abruptly, and it hurt so much. It was grief all over again—not as intense as "real" grief, but grief nonetheless. Stay tuned; there's a lot more.

FINANCES

Chasity

Standing alone doesn't mean I am alone, it means I'm strong enough to handle things all by myself.

—Unknown

During our marriage/time together, finances were not as huge of a stress for us as they are now for me as a widow. I mean, we had our issues, tough times, living paycheck to paycheck, etc., but it did not consume us. For the most part of being together, I was the breadwinner of the family, and Darrell highly respected that. We didn't even have credit card debt, though we had one or two cards for "emergencies." We had the same thoughts on the finances and how things should be done.

But when I became a widow, that one family income became a huge wake-up call for me. And it of course brought on tons of anxieties along with it. I even started opening up credit cards with crazy APRs because I had no other choice for that new refrigerator that broke down or the extra expenses the kids had or maybe the maintenance on the car. You get overwhelmed and think, how can I pay for this or that? And lately, I look into the future and wonder as well about things such as putting Kori through college. Another anxiety I have is the Social Security check that I have been receiving on Kori's behalf. I feel guilty that I have not saved one dime of that because I had to use it to pay bills or just buy everyday, normal things to live. I am terrified of when that goes away in a year and a half. If I can barely make it on what we have now, how the heck am I going to make it without it?

Another part of the financial struggle is the financial planning such my 401(k), etc. I was not strong in this area and still struggle with an understanding of this. Darrell was a huge part in this.

In a nutshell, my financial burdens will be more powerful in the upcoming year and a half, and it is going to be tough. I am going to have to make decisions and possibly make some huge changes that I may not like. I guess in some sense I can look at it as a fresh start: changes, new ways, and things, but I also think it's another confirmation that this is real and Darrell is never coming back. Not to mention, I will be alone, as my son will be off to college. Lots of anxieties have already started and I am not ready for it.

Maureen

You can't see anything properly when your eyes are scarred with tears.

—C. S. Lewis

Finances, sigh! Thinking about my finances brings to mind so many hurtful feelings, hard to think or write about but needed for the healing that needs to take place. The finances really were not a problem with Martin and I until we needed to work together on them. Basically, I had my money, and he had his. I look back on it now and realize that we were totally off base. Our planning was no planning at all. We needed premarital counseling on this and many other issues. But when you know it all, like we thought we did, you can't hear what you need to hear.

Anyway, I was working as a social worker, and Martin worked in community corrections. I would call us lower middle class. When I lost my job, things went to hell in a handbasket. We spent and spent and spent. On what, who knows? Whatever we wanted. Impulse buys, I guess. I made more money than Martin, but at the time, I didn't think that was a problem. It was; he took the attitude that he would just subsidize my income, and I would take care of everything, which I ended up doing and was totally frustrated by.

I financed the house, he obtained one car of his own, and after that, his credit was never good enough to finance again, and I always had to cosign for cars for him. Martin had no respect for credit worthiness and just assumed I would take care of it. He would give me guilt trips if I balked at wanting to cosign for him, saying that I didn't care about anybody but myself and we needed two cars to get by. I always caved and added more burden. I wanted to maintain decent credit, but our spending and lack of budgeting wouldn't allow that. See, I never really knew how to handle my money before marriage, and Martin didn't either; that was a recipe for disaster. We bought a timeshare and actually went to Hilton Head twice. It was nice.

Martin was adopted and grew up in a home with three adopted brothers, and from hearing him talk, it sounded like they lacked at times. His adopted father passed away when Martin was eight. It's weird that he passed away when our oldest daughter, Jordan, was eight. Anyway, when Martin would get his pay, he wanted to do with it what he wanted to do, not caring about any repercussion or thinking about the future. I did all that. I had established my 403(b) plan at work, started Jordan's college fund, and worked on paying down our credit card debt. Martin just wanted stuff. I did too, but he didn't think of the family with his money, just himself. It was very difficult living with a person who I didn't feel was totally turned toward helping the family reach their full potential.

Both of our selfishness ruled in the home. I never remember us in thirteen years of marriage discussing how to allocate money to what was needed. For a period of time, he would give me a percentage to help cover utilities and the mortgage. We never saved. This went on for years, with us always being just over broke. At times, utilities got shut off. It took its toll on our marriage. We didn't trust each other with money. We constantly argued about finances, not realizing that all we needed to do was plan and budget together, and we could have even saved money every month. Although we were not rich by any means, we were not extravagant, and careful planning could have helped us. We were victims of our own pride.

We never truly got along in many other areas of our life. I loved Martin but didn't know how to show it or even tell him. He said he loved me occasionally, but to me, actions speak louder than words. I think he was like me in that regard, not loving himself, so he didn't know how to show me love. Meanwhile, our finances and marriage sunk down into a pit of nothingness.

Martin's health was on a steady decline. I believe he had decided to give up on life and became extremely depressed. He started drinking heavily, going out a few times a week to the bars. Over time, he was gone every night to different bars. Until the last year of his life, he was at the bars all night, and I wouldn't see him until the next morning. I was irate at that and couldn't understand what was going on. He came to me a few times and said that he needed help. I was like, "We should go to AA," but he wouldn't go. I should have called myself; why didn't I? Was it because, like him, I had given up subconsciously on us ever being what God wanted us to be as a married couple? Hmmm, I'll never know the answer.

We needed serious help. We still both had too much pride to come to the table and discuss our issues, and they were not just financial. I really believe our relationship lacked purpose. I mean, why were we together? At that time, we only had our daughter, Jordan, who we had adopted. We had her since she was two days old, straight from the hospital. A nice little family, one would think, but the parents constantly argued and seemed to hate each other at times. We didn't know how to lovingly come back to each other to rekindle what brought us together in the first place.

Back to the cars, I believe both of those got repossessed somewhere in our financial ignorance. The house was going into foreclosure; we were looking for apartments even. Martin passed away before the foreclosure. (Due to the foreclosure backlog with the bank, the house didn't even go into foreclosure until about eighteen months later.) I had just had Mikayla, and we should have been so happy with our new baby, but we weren't. I moved back to the Cleveland, OH, area from Akron two months after he passed away. I could not live in that house where we had lived for nine years. Couldn't sleep there, I was so scared living there. It was a house that was an emotional buy. I financed it, and it was across the street from where Martin grew up. I guess I just wanted to make him happy. We should have waited a few more years, saved more money, and then moved to a better neighborhood, but then we never seemed to do what we should have done financially anyway.

Toward the end, we decided to file for bankruptcy. We didn't have the money to pay the attorney/court costs, but I was able to file In January of 2011, only after Martin had passed away and I obtained a little insurance money. It makes me so sad to think of it. We made our life a shambles, and I believe the stress of it all caused Martin to pass away sooner than he would have if we were getting along.

As I plan our future, I have taken some financial truths from my experience. I know I need to make a certain amount monthly in order for me to feel secure, and I will budget my money and save. I worked jobs for decades, was never happy and never had enough. I believe my financial freedom will come from something I love to do or use and can share with others. Once I am financially free (and I will be) I want to help others to become free also. Financial freedom is a lifestyle, not just a state of being. Everyone has their own definition of what financial freedom is. God is sustaining us until he elevates us.

Khadija

When Ali died, we were in deep debt. Our home was in foreclosure, and because we didn't know when the sheriff was going to show up, we lived with relatives (our lights had been cut off for nonpayment too). We were living with his brother and then moved in with my stepfather. When my stepfather's landlord found out we were staying there, she said we had to move. I knew this news put further stress on Ali, even though he didn't voice it. After sixteen years of living with your spouse, you know them. Not long after that news, he went into the hospital, never to return home. When he died, we were still living with my stepfather. A few weeks after Ali's death, my stepfather's landlord asked when we were leaving. I was devastated and called her to plead with her to let us stay. She was unrelenting, and so in an effort to keep my sanity, I drove the kids to Florida, and we went to Disney World.

As a result of Ali dying, I knew I had the means to do certain things. The fire department paid for his funeral and gave us money to go to Disney, and I would be collecting Social Security and his pension. I was able to pay off some medical bills, credit card debt, and other obligations. Some of our creditors forgave debt (our mechanic and one of his doctors), but others were not so forgiving. The hospital sued me for over $30,000 in medical bills. They did not care that he was deceased; they wanted their money. They removed his name from the lawsuit and instead sued me! I hired a lawyer, who fought the case and won (thank God!). Here I was a newly widowed woman with five children to raise, and I had to figure out where we were going to live, pay off debt, and deal with my own emotions of losing my spouse. It was a crazy time! And as I sit here writing about it, it brings back memories of a time past. It is bringing up emotions of inadequacy, sadness, sorrow, and panic.

After we returned from Disney, it was almost time for school. I called my brother-in-law to ask him if we could move in with him until

I found a place. He told me he would think about it, and I made arrangements to get a hotel room. I paid for the hotel room for two weeks, and my oldest daughter was very unhappy about our situation. She couldn't understand why we didn't just go live with her uncle. I don't remember what I said to her exactly, but I explained we couldn't go there right now and to suck it up. I went to Target and bought two blow-up beds so we could be comfortable in the room. I was so hurt and angry, but at the same time, I knew we had to survive until I could find a place. The next night, my husband's mother called and asked where we were. I told her we were in a hotel room. She asked why we weren't at her son's house, and I told her what he had told me. She hung up with me, and then about ten minutes later, my brother-in-law called and said we could stay with him. The next day I went because I knew the kids would be comfortable, but part of me was still hurt and angry about his first hesitation. This realization of how life was to be would be the first of many eye-opening lessons.

COMPLICATED GRIEF

Chasity

Grief does not fade with the passage of time. We do not realize our losses in an instant; we realize them over years. We do not get over it, but instead go through it, not just once, but as many times as we do. Through grief, we incorporate our losses and weave them into tapestries of our lives so we can stay connected.

—Author Unknown

Complicated grief is a topic I guess to this point, I have been avoiding like the plague. When I think of complicated grief, I think guilt, sadness, anger, and the unknown. I think the perfectionist in me is disappointed in myself too, as to why I did not live the life that I sometimes portrayed or should have. Other times I could care a less what people really think, because let's face it, there are things that go on behind everyone's closed door that we don't know.

It still hurts to think where my relationship was with Darrell when he passed away. It was not at its best. We were together but so far apart. We loved each other but were not in love. We were married but not friends. I think we were growing in two different directions, and I really don't know if we would still be together if he was alive. He was dealing with issues as was I. I think about the insecurities I brought into the marriage and feel guilty about the way I may have treated him or even made him grow apart from me. Did I play a bigger role than him as to why we grew apart? Did I give up in certain aspects? Did I deserve some of the things he said and did to me? Did he do some of the things he did because of me and my actions?

As a spouse, you are already grieving, but there is a part of you that is grieving for answers you will never get, resolutions that should have been resolved, or even just the answers that you will want to know. It's closure you will never get, but you will have to force yourself to think of the positive things and happy memories of where it all started. The not-so-good parts can eat you alive if you let them.

In the beginning, it was hard to focus on the positive, but I wanted and chose to focus on the good, as I want to remember my spouse in a good light, the good times we had, the reason we fell in love and got married, and most importantly I want to share his legacy with his son and for him able to be proud of the man his father was. We all have skeletons in our closet, have issues, are not perfect, and have things going on internally that no one has a clue about. How you move forward and handle those circumstances is what counts. We all have a choice.

Maureen

We're stronger in the places that we've been broken.

—*Ernest Hemingway*

This is my interpretation of complicated grief, which to me means that you lost a loved one through death, but the dynamics of your relationship with that person brings "different" kinds of feelings that are even harder to explain than "regular" grief. There is no such thing as "regular" grief, since grief is individualized to the person experiencing it, but I'm looking for a word to put there.

Meanwhile, I'm writing to Martin as I am today:

Martin, My Dear,

I love you. I'm so sorry I never said it to you when you were with me. See, I couldn't give anything to you that I didn't have to give. Love is a subject that I'm really just getting a grasp of. So while we were together (dating and marriage), it was a foreign topic that I couldn't define or utilize in our life. Martin, I apologize for my lack of knowledge in this area. I know now that I could have had a more positive impact on our lives as a couple. We could have been so great together. I often grieve what we didn't have. I realize that because of your background of being adopted, you had issues regarding being accepted and wanted. It came out in our marriage in trust toward me and how you treated me. We had a "love uncondition," and our "love lack" was our downfall.

I must admit, my sweet, that I've spent the last four and a half years upset about us, what could have been but wasn't. All I knew about being a wife was how to spell it. We both had too much pride. We never served each other. Our purpose was foggy; we were not kind to one another. I didn't honor and respect you; you didn't cherish me. We were always so angry at each other, never on the same page, going different directions in life, playing on opposing teams. I wanted to hide, and you wanted to be with people, which is a normal desire for a human being, and I don't fault you for that. I was just feeling sorry for myself, having a grand time in my "pitiful parties."

I regret not letting you lead our family. Maybe I mean I regret not knowing what the proper order of things for our family to run smoothly was. You seemed content to let me do everything, and I was overwhelmed, tired, and just plain mad.

When our financial world crumbled due to job loss and years of overspending and not planning, what was left of our marriage pushed us apart. You gave up on your health and our family. You sought out solace for our issues in alcohol, despair, and another woman. You said you wanted a divorce while I was pregnant with your child. I was praying for God to make us whole again, but we were not reconciled to each other, we couldn't find our way home, which would have been us united as one, as married couples should be. We took too much emotionally and did not deposit into each other, leaving our marriage totally bankrupt.

Martin, as your wife, I should have loved you no matter what. I should have worked with you, instead of against you. I should have been supportive of you. I was always late, and you were furious about that, since being on time was your forte. You even said that whenever you are late it's because someone made you late, and I was usually the culprit. I didn't do it on purpose, but it was passive aggression on my part toward you.

I could not cook, and you loved to eat! That was a huge problem, but you could cook very well, so that was a huge help. I should have been more open to learning to cook, but my focus was more on going to work and bringing money in to pay the bills. We both needed a huge dose of humility and Ephesians 5 and a marital intervention plan or the MIP.

I will say that we withstood a lot: your mother's passing, my mother's passing, job loss, car repossessions, foreclosure, job hatred, adoption loss, adoption of a child, fertility issues, the birth of a child under extreme financial stress, the death of a child. Martin, our baby died, and we were still together! That speaks volumes to our commitment to each other. We were content in our marriage until your health declined and our financial debacle (2007).

I guess what I have to say is that I've forgiven you, god has forgiven me, and finally, I had to forgive myself for not knowing what I didn't know about marriage and being a wife. I'm healing.

You know, Martin, when I moved back to Cleveland after living in Akron for seventeen years, I joined a wonderful, loving church, Providence. We had visited there a few times, and you even said you liked the people in the congregation. Anyway, it seemed that as soon as joined, the pastor started doing a marital series. I was upset for about a month on that. This was like August of 2010, and you had just passed away in April of 2010. I even left in the middle of one of the sermons, just grabbed the kids and left. Yes, I did! I remember thinking, "Lord, why do I need to hear this marital *stuff? My husband just died! No one is ever gonna want me anyway!" Yes, those were my exact thoughts. I was a woman in shambles, very unwell.*

I haven't even mentioned the kids. I talk about them elsewhere. Martin, I believe you would be so proud of me. I started hearing you after you passed away. I'm what you dreamed I would be: loving, full of confidence, outgoing, a submissive flame, wanting to work together with whom I'm united with. Martin, I finally learned to smile. You always asked me why I never ever smiled. It was because of what was going on inside of me, how I felt about me. Now I feel that there is nothing I can't do! I am unstoppable!

Martin, I leave you first with a kiss (muah!), then with this: Our marriage had its ups (our beautiful daughters), downs and sideways. Such is life, but I'm not bitter about it. Ours was a bittersweet marriage as some are, but as I move forward, I'll use our marriage as a canvas on which to paint the portrait of the rest of my journey. I believe that will include another marriage. Martin, I know you would understand. Our marriage was the foundation, the fundamentals, the classroom for me to get it wrong and get it right. Deep down in my spirit I know that someone, somewhere is out there for me to come together as one with. I call him my Mr. Someday, with whom I'll be able to lovingly apply what I learned in our marriage.

Thank you, Martin. I love you.

Your wife on earth,

Victoria

(When I first met Martin, he asked me what my name was, and I told him Victoria, which is my middle name. I wanted to feel victorious in life and went by that name for the time that Martin and I were together.)

Khadija

2006

We were having problems before he got sick, but put everything on the back burner when he had surgery and went through chemo. Once he was back to work and focused on his career again, things were semi-normal. We started drifting apart again. I was in school but unhappy at home. He was working a lot, and we were two ships passing in the night. We still did things with the kids, went to family functions, and paid bills, but our relationship was at an impasse. I decided in October 2006 that I was moving and taking the kids with me to Florida. I felt like he chose his career over me. I had sacrificed so much before when he went to school to be an electrician. Now, here he was pursuing another career, and what about me? What about what I wanted to do? Our kids were getting older, and all were in school. I now had more time to pursue what I wanted to do. I didn't feel like I was getting the support I needed to pursue my dreams.

I had planned to just and up and leave and not even tell him. One day I was talking to a family friend via Yahoo! Messenger about me leaving, and left the window open. Ali came home, found the window open, and saw the messages. He came to me to talk about it, and we both decided that what would be best was that I would go to Florida first and establish myself and then bring the kids down. Our separation was quite amicable. We had a separation agreement in place, and he wished me well. And off I went to Florida in December 2006.

I spent four months there, getting myself together. I looked for jobs, found a small apartment, and was finally on my way to financial and emotional independence. For many years, I was a wife and a mother; now it was time to find out who Khadija was.

During this four-month separation, Ali and I became close. I would come to Jersey from time to time because we had a property to sell, and our primary house was in foreclosure, and we were trying to sell it before the bank took over. I realized that walking away from a sixteen-year marriage wasn't going to be as easy as I had previously thought. We had so much unfinished business—both financially and emotionally.

Ali and I frequently communicated during our separation, mostly via e-mail and occasionally on the phone. He would keep me abreast of the kids with pictures and email updates. I don't remember when our communication started to pick up more frequently, but we went from talking occasionally to talking every day. It was like discovering your best friend all over again. We had been high school sweethearts who started out as friends anyway. We talked about everything: the kids, business, and work. He even helped me with my resume when I had a major interview with a prominent company. God knew what He was doing in bringing us back together near the end. I am grateful that I got to spend time getting to know myself in those four months away. But I am most grateful that I came back home.

LESSONS LEARNED

Chasity

Time doesn't heal all wounds, we just get better at it.

—The Queen Mother after the death of King Edward

What I learned:

- Asking for help is okay.

- You need GOD

- Get books, read and connect

- Journal and write

- Take care of yourself even if its hard.

- It's okay to cry and multiple times a day- its not a sign of weakness.

- Accepting comfort is okay.

- Counseling does help. It provides tools/resources to help you get through and to teach you how to handle grief. Everyone is different.

- Helping others helps.

- It takes time, whatever it may be: learning new things, adjusting to the new life.

- Moving forward is okay.

- Reinventing a new normal is not easy, but it is worth it.

- You are stronger than you think you are.

- Saying no is okay.

- It is okay to make mistakes and wrong decisions. We are not perfect.

- Not everyone will truly understand your journey, even when they say they will/do.

- There is someone you can connect to that will understand.

- Life is fragile and can change in a second.

- You must be kind to yourself and not so critical.

- Everyone grieves differently.

- Grief comes in waves.

- You may come to more peace with your loved one gone, but there will always be a hole in your heart, and you will always miss their presence.

- Baby steps is sometimes all it takes. The bigger picture, the rest of "it" will come in time. As long as you're moving, it is better than doing nothing at all.

- Do not take people's comments and/or actions personally.

- Do not make significant decisions/changes for at least a couple years. (Most people say one year. I think it's longer.)

- Life goes on no matter your circumstance.

- You will lose friendships, people close to you unexpectedly.

- People will judge.

- People will have many assumptions of your widowhood journey.

- You will digress and then progress and digress again and progress. It is a roller coaster at times.

- You will cry a lot.

- No matter how many years it has been, you will still deal with grief.

- It's okay to mention their name. We want to hear it; we want you to share stories.

- People avoid Grief like the plague, makes them uncomfortable

- People will always have their opinions on how you grieve

Maureen

*I found it **fascinating** that, at my **lowest,** I felt god planting the seed in me for **service** in the **ministry of love** to other hurting people.*

—*Maureen Bobo*

Lessons Learned

You **are** stronger than you could **ever** imagine.

You **cannot** go home again.

You **create** your own normal.

Some people **care**, and some people only **pretend** to care; know the difference.

I **cannot** stop life from going on.

You **will** feel better at some point; it **cannot** be rushed.

I **need** others who can relate to my feelings in my life.

I am **still** becoming.

I **won't** always let grief lead my choices.

I **need** to educate people about grief.

If I had **known** better, I would have **done** better.

I **miss** people when they leave.

My children **will** be okay.

Talking **helps.**

Isolation **hurts.**

71

I've become **patient** with people.

I **want** to hear what people have to say.

I **can** smile again.

My **dreams** have not died.

I have **survived** the most tragic thing imaginable.

I believe I have **survivor instincts**. They're going to help me **thrive.**

The stares don't bother me anymore.

I am loveable.

I will love again.

I am alive.

I've **discovered** my **greatness.**

From Facebook Notes October 2012

There she goes reminiscing again, SMH. It was twenty years ago this month that I met Martin, in October of 1992. I don't remember the day, perhaps the 13th or so; all I know is that I was watching a Browns game and he called. A mutual friend had given him my number, and we started talking, and the rest, as they say, is history.

The above is a note I wrote a few years back, to all the Maureens out there. It is about what I learned from Martin's death and the process I have gone through. I look back and say that I was such a baby, LOL; all I needed was a diaper.

Martin was what I call an off-brand person, not your typical Coke or Pepsi, unique, different, unusual. I guess, I'm drawn to people who are different or off-brand, maybe because I think I'm that way too, not sure. I realize I like people who don't follow the standard patterns of life. But anyway, one might look at Martin and say, "Offensive line," but you'd be wrong, LOL. Martin never played football. He played baseball as a child, he didn't even like sports, LOL.

I find that weird, that we got together at all. How can a man in northeast Ohio, the cradle of football civilization, not like at least football? He liked the professional wrestling, LOL, and here I am, sports fan since about the age of seven, lol! I would say about 97 percent of women don't even watch football, let alone like it. I'm in the 3 percent. On Sunday afternoons when I was watching Browns games, Martin would take Jordan out to the park, to eat, or visiting people; it was nice. All the different sporting events I would be watching, alone, and he would find something to do.

Wow, he had his westerns, especially John Wayne. Because of him, I watch westerns now. There are some great ones: *The Searchers*, *The Oxbow Incident*, to name a few. We would come together on old movies. We both loved *On Borrowed Time* and *To Kill A Mockingbird*. He had his his comic books. I have about 150 of 'em in the storage closet, from the 70s–80s. He kept them in good condition, and he got offended when people didn't know which comic went to Marvel and which went to DC Comics, so I used to mess 'em up on purpose so he would school me on my comic book character history, lol. He had his Food Network, and he loved to cook.

It's a wonder how two people get together and change each other to different viewpoints and ideas. I feel like we were so incomplete. We didn't get to come full circle in our relationship, and I feel cheated, SMH, cut off in some sort of way. I get confused by trying to figure out the reasons for things happening, so I stopped the wondering whys. All I know is that I met a man, I married a man, I made a life with a man, and I buried a man, all in about a twenty-year span of time. I know that part of my life is over, but can you ever really stop thinking about a person that you were as one with? I say no. Therein lies the dilemma: I have to move forward, but I can't stop looking back, SMH. I am not over, far from it; we'll see what happens.

Khadija

I had the most difficult time writing this because, frankly, many good lessons have come out of becoming a widow at the age of thirty-five. I know that sounds crazy to you, the reader, because you are most likely in the early stages of your grief. Everything is turned upside down and topsy-turvy. You don't know if you're coming or going. Life may feel meaningless, and the pain (especially at night) is unbearable. Here is what I learned:

• You are much stronger than you have ever been in your life. It may not feel like it now, but you are.

• Your children are resilient and will be okay. You don't feel that is possible right now, but they will be okay.

• Your friends and family will change. You will lose some people, but you will gain some new friends that will be like family and be there for you in ways you couldn't imagine.

• The only way to heal is to let time do its job. Yes, pray. Yes, talk, journal, cry, scream, and shout. Let time be your friend.

• It's okay to express your feelings. Seek out those who will listen to you without judgment.

• Death makes people uncomfortable. Forgive them for not wanting to hear you talk about your spouse or grief, forgive them for not calling like they used to, forgive them for avoiding you. That is their stuff, not yours.

• Drugs and alcohol will only mask your pain. The grief monster is one sneaky SOB and will wait until you are sober or no longer high and still show up.

• You will grow in ways you never thought. Out of your tragedy, you will become the greatest version of you!

• J. California Cooper said it best: "Life is short but wide." Cram as much as you can in the time given to you!

• And like Dory says in *Finding Nemo*, "Just keep swimming!" You will make it!

BIOGRAPHIES

Chasity

Chasity Williams is currently a Practice Coordinator for a Management Consulting Firm in Dallas, TX. Chasity was a stay-at-home mom for several years, until she decided to transition into the workforce full time. She was employed in the administrative field with several leading companies, where she supported executive-level leaders and managed office practices in diverse industries. Chasity met her late husband at the young age of eighteen. In June of 2009, her life would forever change when she lost her husband suddenly in a drowning at the age of thirty-four years old. Finding out who she was again, raising her son and living life to the fullest even after this tragedy was a mission she was eager to accomplish. Chasity and Darrell have one son together who is now attending college and pursuing his dreams in Business Marketing and Management. Chasity enjoys volunteering, sporting events, writing, and spending time with her family and friends.

Maureen

Maureen Bobo is a Christ follower, love advocate, social worker, and mompreneur. Her ministries include grief, singles, and health and wellness. Maureen is a single parent of two daughters ages fourteen and six. She became a single parent on April 7, 2010, when her husband of thirteen years, Martin Bobo, passed away of chronic heart disease at the age of forty-five. The children at that time were ages eight years and two months old.

The grief from that tragedy led Maureen to develop The Beautiful Stones Ministries, in which the goal is to provide love and support to the grieving heart. Maureen is also involved in singles ministry development at her church. She believes that singles need to be nurtured and cultivated in the season that they are in so they can thrive in life. Maureen has completed three half marathons and has a goal to complete a half marathon in every state. She has a message for people: "Be your own superhero, and make your own self proud through intentional self-care." She plans to encourage people worldwide to rock their inner athlete to the core and become unleashed!

Through her life story, Maureen wants to encourage and inspire people to not only dream but dream big, by putting their faith in flight and loving themselves and others.

Visit her website: www.healthaliciouscoffee.myorganogold.com

Khadija

As a healer, speaker, and teacher, Khadija uses her passion for advocating for women in the matters of money, prosperity, and abundance. She is the CEO of Evolutionary Woman and radio host of Evolutionary Woman Radio. Her passion for coaching stems from triumphing over the tragedy in her own life. In 2007, she found herself a single mom to five children after losing her husband to colon cancer. Overnight, she had to figure it out!

Visit her website www.evolutionarywoman.net, or listen to archived shows of Evolutionary Woman Radio at

www.blogtalkradio.com/evolutionarywomanradio.

PREVENTATIVE ACTION AND RESOURCES

This chapter is dedicated to share preventative action and resources related to our husband's deaths. Maureen, Chasity, and Khadija cannot stress enough the importance of getting check-ups, knowing your family history (heart disease, colon cancer, etc.), and learning and practicing water safety to help prevent drowning. Holding yourself and your loved ones accountable for the health and education of topics could just save a life. We hope you find these resources helpful.

Below are a list of links to these resources:

Water Safety

No matter if you are young or old, in the greatest shape, a great swimmer or even if you want to just take a quick dip in the water, please take time out to educate yourself and practice water safety consistently. WEAR A LIFE JACKET- it saves lives! I wish my loved one did.

Red Cross Website:

http://www.redcross.org/get-help/prepare-for-emergencies/types-of-emergencies/water-safety

http://watersafety.usace.army.mil

http://www.bobber.info (kid interactive)

Heart Health

Heart disease is the No. 1 killer for all Americans, and stroke is also a leading cause of death. As frightening as those statistics are the risks of getting those diseases are even higher for African-Americans.

"Get checked, then work with your medical professional on your specific risk factors and the things that you need to do to take care of your personal health," said Winston Gandy, M.D., a cardiologist and chief medical marketing officer with the Piedmont Heart Institute in Atlanta and a volunteer with the American Heart Association. www.heart.org. For your family, for yourself. Please know your risk factors. Below are helpful links to learn more about Heart Disease THE SILENT KILLER...

http://www.heart.org/.../Make-the-Effort-to-Prevent-Heart

http://www.heart.org/.../African-Americans-and-Heart-Disease

https://www.goredforwomen.org/.../live.../prevent-heart-disease/

Colorectal Cancer

Colorectal cancer occurs more frequently in African-American men and women than in any other racial group in the United States, according to the American Cancer Society. Death rates from the disease are also higher in African-Americans than in other racial groups.

It's unclear why these differences exist, but access to and attitudes toward prevention and treatment may offer some explanation. Several studies have found that African-American patients are more likely to be diagnosed after the cancer has spread beyond the colon, making it more difficult to treat successfully. Another study found that African-Americans were half as likely as Caucasians to have undergone colonoscopy screening, even after accounting for differences in education, income, and health insurance status. In addition, African-Americans with colorectal cancer are less likely than Caucasian patients to receive recommended surgical treatment and therapies.

Fortunately, colorectal cancer is highly treatable if caught early enough. If you're older than fifty or at risk for colorectal cancer, you should ask your doctor about getting screened—it could save your life.

Source: https://www.fredhutch.org/en/events/cancer-in-our-communities/african-americans-and-cancer.html#colon

Note: I want to add that my husband was thirty-four when the cancer was found. Had he not gone in for a physical for the fire department, it would have never been discovered. Unbeknownst to him, he had a family history. If you have a family history, I strongly urge you to get testing before the age of fifty.

Visit http://www.cancer.org/index to find local screenings in your area.

RELATABLE QUOTES

We, The Unwelcome Committee found that these following quotes were comforting and relatable to our journey through widowhood. We wanted to share them with you in the hopes that you would find some hope in them too.

You can do the impossible because you have been through the unimaginable.
— Christina Rasmussen

Those we love don't go away, they walk beside us every day, unseen, unheard, but always here, still loved and missed every day and very dear.
— Unknown

It's not about forcing happiness, it's about not letting sadness win. The Wonder Years

Progress always involves risk. You can't steal second base and keep your foot on first.
— Frederick Wilcox

Challenges are what makes life interesting; overcoming them is what makes life meaningful.
— Joshua J. Marine

Faith is taking the first step even when you don't see the whole staircase.
—MLK

Grief does not come in one size fits all; we each are unique and so is our grief.

— Unknown

The moment may be temporary, but the memory is forever.

— Bud Meyer

Time doesn't heal all wounds, we just get better at it.

—The Queen Mother after the death of King Edward.

Grief is like rain. Sometimes it only drizzles, but other times it pours so much you feel like you're going to drown in it.

Unknown

Grief does not fade with the passage of time. We do not realize our losses in an instant; we realize them over years. We do not get over it, but instead go through it, not just once, but as many times as we do. Through grief, we incorporate our losses and weave them into tapestries of our lives so we can stay connected.

Unknown

You never know how strong you are, until being strong is the only choice you have.

Bob Marley

I won't let grief lead my choices.

Maureen Bobo

Helping others helps me.

Khadija Ali

Do not make decisions for a couple of years. It's more than a year.

Chasity

"For I know the plans I have for you," says the Lord. "They are plans for good and not for evil, to give you a future and a hope. In those days when you pray, I will listen. You will find me when you seek me, if you look for me in earnest." "Yes," says the Lord, "I will be found by you and I will end your

slavery and restore your fortunes, and gather you out of the nations where I sent you and bring you back home again to your own land."
Jeremiah 29:11-14

Your beautifully messy, complicated story matters. Tell it.
Quote from Elizabeth Berrien Respite's page

Writing a book is like driving a car at night; you can only see to the end of your headlights, but you can make the whole trip that way.
E. L. Doctorow

Grief is like a jigsaw puzzle. Some people get all the edge pieces together first and work from the outside in. Others dump everything out on the table at once and jump right into the middle. Some never open the box at all. They just look at the picture on the outside and wonder why what's inside the box doesn't match or make sense. You meet a lot of people when you start a jigsaw puzzle. Some are full of advice, or they may try to make the puzzle look the way it ought to be instead of the way it is. But, once in a while, you meet someone who shares their own finished puzzle and helps you to make some sense of yours. Then you find it is not as hard as before. Some of the pieces fit together more easily, and you sigh with relief, and remember.
Victoria Guthrie

Quotes Galore

While going through the fire, you are being shaped for significance. You go from "Why me, Lord?" to "Here I am, Lord, use me!"
Maureen Bobo

Grief is like the ocean, it comes in waves, ebbing and flowing. Sometimes the water is calm, and sometimes it is overwhelming. All we can do is learn to swim.
Vickie Harrison

After being broken into one thousand pieces, I realized only God's love could heal me one piece at a time.
Maureen Bobo

I always saw the light at the end of the tunnels. Sometimes it was really dim, but it never went out. Now it shines bright. I feel its warmth on my cheeks, and I start smiling.
Maureen Bobo

There is absolutely not a time limit on grief, so don't rush yourself or let others rush you.
Unknown

Love when you're ready, not when you're lonely.
Unknown

Yes, I've changed. Pain does that to people.
Unknown

Don't hide your scars. Wear them as proof that God heals.
Unknown

When you come out of the storm, you won't be the same person that walked in. That's what the storm is all about.
Haruki Murakami

Out of suffering have emerged the strongest souls.
Khalil Gilbran

Grief is as individual as a snowflake.
Julia Cook

Don't be ashamed of your story. It will inspire others.
Unknown

The people who are meant to be in your life are the ones who know how to gently wait for you to heal.
Unknown

Everyone sees what you appear to be. Few experience what you really are.
Niccolo Machiavelli

The Lord is close to the broken-hearted and saves those who are crushed in spirit.
Psalm 34:18 (NIV)

You can't see anything properly when your eyes are scarred with tears.
C. S. Lewis

We're stronger in the places that we've been broken.
Ernest Hemingway

Grief is the last act of love we have to give to those we have loved. Where there is deep grief, there was great love.
Unknown

The most beautiful stones have been tossed by the wind, washed by the water, and polished to brilliance by life's strongest storms.
Unknown

He comforts us in all our troubles so that we can comfort others. When they are troubled, we will be able to give them the same comfort god has given us.
2 Corinthians 1:4 (NLT)

Made in the USA
Charleston, SC
25 August 2016